THE ART OF WOODWORKING

HOME WORKSHOP

THE ART OF WOODWORKING

HOME WORKSHOP

TIME-LIFE BOOKS
ALEXANDRIA, VIRGINIA

ST. REMY PRESS
MONTREAL • NEW YORK

THE ART OF WOODWORKING was produced by
ST. REMY PRESS

PUBLISHER	Kenneth Winchester
PRESIDENT	Pierre Léveillé
Series Editor	Pierre Home-Douglas
Series Art Director	Francine Lemieux
Senior Editors	Marc Cassini (Text)
	Heather Mills (Research)
Art Directors	Normand Boudreault, Luc Germain,
	Solange Laberge
Designers	Jean-Guy Doiron, Michel Giguère
Research Editor	Jim McRae
Picture Editor	Christopher Jackson
Writers	Andrew Jones, Rob Lutes
Contributing Illustrators	Gilles Beauchemin, Rolland Bergera,
	Jean-Pierre Bourgeois, Michel Blais,
	Nicole Chartier, Ronald Durepos,
	Philippe Gauvreau, Gérard Mariscalchi,
	Jacques Perrault, Robert Paquet,
	James Thérien
Administrator	Natalie Watanabe
Production Manager	Michelle Turbide
System Coordinator	Jean-Luc Roy
Photographer	Robert Chartier

Time-Life Books is a division of Time-Life Inc.,
a wholly owned subsidiary of
THE TIME INC. BOOK COMPANY

TIME-LIFE BOOKS

President	John D. Hall
Vice-President	Nancy K. Jones
Editor-in-Chief	Thomas H. Flaherty
Director of Editorial Resources	Elise D. Ritter-Clough
Marketing Director	Regina Hall
Editorial Director	Lee Hassig
Consulting Editor	John R. Sullivan
Production Manager	Marlene Zack

THE CONSULTANTS

Jon Arno is a consultant, cabinetmaker and freelance writer who lives in Troy, Michigan. He also conducts seminars on wood identification and early American furniture design.

Giles Miller-Mead taught advanced cabinetmaking at Montreal technical schools for more than ten years. A native of New Zealand, he has worked as a restorer of antique furniture.

Joseph Truini is Senior Editor of *Home Mechanix* magazine. A former Shop and Tools Editor of *Popular Mechanics*, he has worked as a cabinetmaker, home improvement contractor and carpenter.

Home Workshop
    p. cm.—(The Art of Woodworking)
Includes index.
ISBN 0-8094-9920-7. (trade)
ISBN 0-8094-9921-5 (lib)
1. Woodshops.
2. Woodwork--Equipment and supplies.
I. Time-Life Books. II. Series
TT152.H6 1993
684' .08—dc20   92-6821
                                      CIP

For information about any Time-Life book, please call 1-800-621-7026, or write:
Reader Information
Time-Life Customer Service
P.O. Box C-32068
Richmond, Virginia
23261-2068

CONTENTS

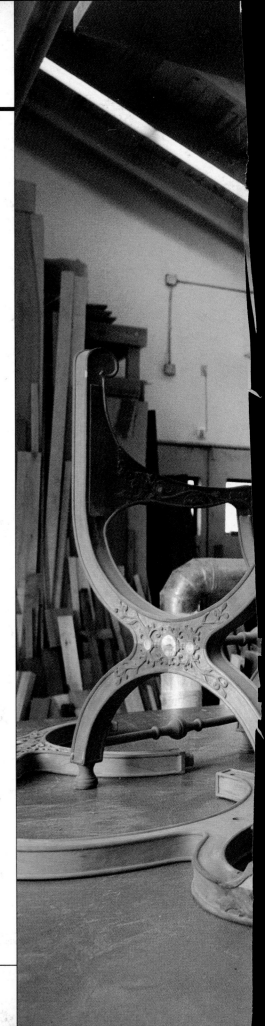

Peter Axtell talks about planning his
DREAM WORKSHOP

I started woodworking around 1974 in England, where I was playing rock music and needed a hobby to help me unwind from the rigors of the road. My shop at the time was just big enough for a workbench, a radial arm saw, and not much else. I remember constantly bumping things into the low ceiling.

When my wife and I moved back to America I was offered a job in a local wood-shop run by a friend of mine. It was there that I began to acquire a feel for how a shop should be laid out. After a few years with my friend I left and set up my own shop in our three-car garage. I soon learned what worked and what didn't. When it came time to plan a shop from scratch, I sought out my local woodworking organization, which turned out to be a fountain of information. I studied lots of shops in my area and asked hundreds of questions about what people liked and what they wanted to change in their own shops.

I saw one place in particular that seemed the best for my needs and settled on that as my model. My budget allowed me 1,500 square feet, so that was one limit set. Light—both natural and artificial—was a major consideration. I placed my building and planned the windows to take maximum advantage of the abundant sunlight in northern California. I was also determined to have a wood floor. I quickly found out that a hardwood floor would be too expensive so I used 1⅛-inch tongue-and-groove plywood and epoxy paint, which have held up very well over the last nine years.

I figured out the floor plan on graph paper and cut out scale drawings of all my machines as well as areas for plywood storage, office space, and a spray booth. It is important to allow enough space around your machines, so I spent considerable time movings things around and testing different scenarios.

The crawl space under my shop has extra clearance because I chose to run my dust collection pipe under the floor, which has allowed me to keep the whole ceiling space clear and airy. One of the best investments I made was in super-insulating the whole shop—floors, walls, and ceiling, which has made it easier to keep the place warm in winter and cool in summer.

I put a lot of thought and research into my shop and there isn't much I would change except for one thing: I wish I had built it bigger. But that is a common complaint. It seems that you can never have too much space.

Peter Axtell builds fine furniture at his shop in Sonoma County, California.

Martha Collins discusses
SHOP STORAGE

I make jewelry from exotic wood and dyed veneer. Some pieces have as many as 800 bits of wood in them, combining the colors and textures of various rare woods with brightly hued veneers. Being able to find some offbeat screw or fastener when I need it, or knowing where to retrieve that wonderful small chunk of rosewood that I've been saving for 10 years isn't a luxury; it's a necessity. Through the years, I have learned that the strength of a workshop depends on proper organization and storage.

I have four distinct "storage areas" in my shop. The infeed and outfeed tables of my radial arm saw hold scrap wood and less frequently used tools. My jewelry storage bench holds all the machined and milled exotic woods and dyed veneers. The 4-by-8 outfeed table on the table saw houses a variety of items: work in progress, exotic lumber, furniture pads, and leftovers from the jewelry-making process.

The most important storage area is in the main workbench and tool chest area. This is the heart of my shop. I keep everything from screws and screwdrivers to planes and hinges in cabinets close to the bench. All of the hand and power tools that I use regularly are kept in my main chest, which is featured in the photograph.

The chest is 6 feet high and 4 feet wide. In the upper section, I store everything from hammers and one set of chisels in the left-hand door to files, screwdrivers, and planes in the right-hand section. The five drawers in the center are filled with wrenches and bits of all kinds—spurs, twists, and Forstners. I assembled the drawers with dovetail joints, a satisfying effort that only adds to the pleasure of putting things away.

The left-hand door in the bottom section of the chest holds all my measuring and marking tools; the right-hand door houses a set of pliers along with my handsaws. The cubbyholes are home to my portable power tools—circular saws, saber saws, router, sander, cordless drills, pneumatic tools, and so on.

The tools in my chest have changed over the years. Fifteen years ago I had only one cordless drill; now I have three. But my chest has been able to adapt and accommodate all the new tools—each with its own specific place.

Martha Collins designs and makes fine jewelry and furniture in her workshop near Sequim, Washington. Her husband, luthier Richard Schneider, works in an adjoining shop.

Leonard Lee on

THE VALUE OF A WORKBENCH

Aworkshop can be anywhere you can fit a solid surface. A retired carver friend built a superb workshop in the linen closet of his apartment. He only had to open the closet door, pull out a stool, and go to work. Everything he needed was fitted into a space of less than 10 square feet.

I built the small cherry bench in the photograph to fit an awkward alcove in my office that measures only 23 by 37 inches. For years I had been using my desk as a makeshift workbench and I was frustrated by both the lack of any decent clamping system and enough clear work surface. The desk is often as cluttered as the bookcase in the background.

With the workbench in place, I can now clamp wood for testing saws, chisels, bits, and so on, without knocking a coffee cup to the floor or spilling papers everywhere. The bench is also just the right height for using an inspection microscope, an invaluable tool for analyzing failures and successes in the world of sharp edges.

The bench occupies an otherwise unusable space next to a doorway. Since the floor space next to it can be used only for foot traffic, the bench only adds to the usability of my office; it does not detract anything. Incidentally, the bench was pulled out of the alcove for this photo.

More important than its utility, my bench adds a wonderfully relaxing and humanizing element. Like many people, I tire quickly of administrative detail. With a workbench handy, I can get up from my desk, wander over to the bench and tinker with tools for a while. It is like a mini-vacation in the middle of the day.

The humanizing part comes from surrounding yourself with things you like. I like everything about woodworking. My office is filled with old tools as well as books about their history and use. To add a workbench to the general clutter is just another layer to the cocoon. The world looks much better when viewed from an office with a workbench in it.

Leonard Lee is the president of Veritas Tools and Lee Valley Tools in Ottawa, Canada, manufacturers and retailers of fine woodworking hand tools. He is also the publisher and executive editor of Woodcuts, *a magazine that focuses on the history and techniques of woodworking.*

SAFETY

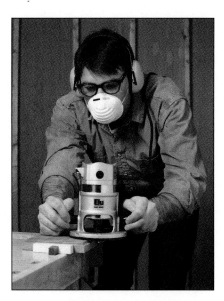

Personal safety gear is one insurance against injury. Here, a woodworker routs a groove in a drawer front, wearing safety glasses, a dust mask, and ear muffs.

For most woodworkers, the home workshop is a peaceful refuge, where craft gives shape to creative ideas. It is also the place where accidents may occur, owing to the very nature of the activity. But the likelihood of mishap can be reduced by a few simple precautions. First, an informed woodworker is a safe woodworker. Read the owner's manuals supplied with all your tools. Before starting a job, make sure you know how to use the safety accessories that are designed to protect you from injury while working with a tool.

Most accidents are the result of carelessness or inattention—failure to use a safety guard when cutting a board on a table saw, face jointing stock with bare hands (rather than with a push block), or using a router without safety goggles. Refer to the safety tips on page 14 for ways of avoiding some of the more common accidents in the shop.

Although the big stationary machines receive most of the attention from safety-conscious woodworkers, there are other potential sources of danger that, though less apparent, cannot be ignored. Many finishing products, particularly those containing solvents, can be toxic, although their effects may only become apparent after years of prolonged exposure. Certain species of wood can cause allergic or toxic reactions in some people. Page 15 presents information on choosing safe finishing products and on the possible health effects of some wood species. Safety goggles, rubber gloves, and a rubber apron are good standard attire for any finishing job, especially if you are spraying a finish or mixing and applying caustic chemicals.

Fire is another shop hazard. Smoke detectors are an invaluable defence, providing valuable time for you to control the blaze *(page 16)*. Keep a fire extinguisher rated ABC in your shop and know how to use it. One of the leading causes of fire is improper wiring. Whether you are building a shop from scratch or revamping an existing space, electrical safety should be a priority *(page 17)*.

No shop should be without the personal safety gear illustrated on page 18. You can easily make some safety devices, such as push sticks, push blocks, and featherboards *(page 20)*. But do not become complacent about the security they will provide. All the safety equipment in the world cannot make a shop accident-free. Safety is foremost a matter of attitude—a confidence in using the machines combined with a healthy respect for the power these tools wield.

Even with the best efforts at prevention, accidents still occur. Bits may break, boards split, shavings fly and all too often find a victim. Being prepared and taking prompt action can help minimize further damage. Take a first-aid course, keep a well-stocked first-aid kit on hand in the shop *(page 23)* and be ready to administer medical aid when necessary.

There are many safety devices that can minimize the risk of using power tools. The table saw in this photo features a plastic shield that covers the blade; the splitter and the anti-kickback pawl protect against binding and kickback. A hold-down device presses the workpiece flat on the table and firmly against the fence. A push stick allows the woodworker to feed the stock into the blade while keeping fingers well away from the cutting edge.

ACCIDENT PREVENTION

SAFETY TIPS

GENERAL

• Make sure workshop lighting and ventilation are adequate.

• Keep children, onlookers, and pets away from the work area.

• Concentrate on the job; do not rush or take shortcuts. Never work when you are tired, stressed, or have been drinking alcohol or using medications that induce drowsiness.

• Find a comfortable stance; avoid overreaching.

• Keep your work area clean and tidy; clutter can lead to accidents.

HAND TOOLS

• Use the appropriate tool for the job; do not try to make a tool do something for which it was not designed.

• When possible, cut away from yourself rather than toward your body.

• Keep tools clean and sharp.

POWER TOOLS

• Wear appropriate safety gear: safety glasses or face shield and hearing protection. If there is no dust collection system, wear a dust mask. For allergenic woods, such as ebony, use a respirator.

• Read your owner's manual carefully before operating any tool.

• Tie back long hair and avoid loose-fitting clothing. Remove rings and other jewelry that can catch in moving parts.

• Unplug a tool before performing setup or installation operations.

• Whenever possible, clamp down the workpiece, leaving both hands free to perform an operation.

• Keep your hands well away from a turning blade or bit.

• Turn off a tool if it produces an unfamiliar vibration or noise; have the tool serviced before resuming operations.

• Do not use a tool if any part of it is worn or damaged.

FINISHING

• Do not eat, drink, or smoke when using finishing products.

• Avoid exposure to organic solvents if you are pregnant or breast-feeding.

• Install at least one smoke detector on the ceiling of your shop above potential fire hazards; keep a fully charged ABC fire extinguisher nearby.

• Never store solvents or chemicals in unmarked containers. Chemical solutions should always be stored in dark glass jars to shield them from light, which may change their composition.

• Store finishing products in a locked cabinet.

•To prevent eye injury, wear safety goggles, and don rubber gloves when working with caustic or toxic finishing products.

• Do not flush used solvents down the drain. Consult the Yellow Pages to find out who handles chemical disposal in your area, or check with your local fire department.

SHOP TIP

Disabling a power tool
To prevent unauthorized use of a power tool, slip the bolt of a mini-padlock through one of the tines in the power cord plug. The lock will make it impossible to plug in the tool. If you are using a keyed lock, store the keys out of the way in a cupboard or drawer that can be locked.

WORKING WITH SAFE FINISHES

Although a number of high-quality water-based finishes have become available recently, solvent-based finishing products are still widely used, and considered superior for some applications. Thus woodworkers must learn to protect themselves against the health hazards associated with organic solvents. Organic solvents can have a number of health effects. Short-term use can result in ailments ranging from headaches and nausea to skin and eye irritation. With extended use, many solvents are known to damage the central nervous system or respiratory tract. Some glycol ethers are suspected of causing birth defects, while other solvents, like methylene chloride, have been linked with cardiac arrest.

Solvents can be absorbed into the bloodstream in a number of ways: after being inhaled, or ingested along with food left in the shop, absorbed through the skin, or swallowed when vapors settle in saliva. Most solvent-based finishes are unlikely to cause harm when used occasionally, and are only poisonous if swallowed. But you still need to be aware of the combination and concentration of organic solvents in a particular finish if you plan to use the product in large quantities or over an extended period of time. The chart below lists the solvents contained in a variety of finishing products and assesses the relative toxicity of each one. Be sure to choose the safest product for the job at hand.

TOXIC SOLVENTS

FINISHING PRODUCT	SOLVENT
Wood filler (paste and liquid)	Petroleum naphtha,* mineral spirits,* acetone,** methyl ethyl ketone,** methyl isopropanol,** isobutyl ketone***
Stains (aniline, wiping, NGR, gel and glazing stains; color pigments)	Ethanol,* mineral spirits,* toluene,*** xylene,*** methanol,*** glycol ethers***
Shellacs (white and orange)	Ethanol,* methanol***
Lacquers (spray and brush, sanding sealers)	Acetone,** methyl ethyl ketone,** isopropanol,** methanol,*** xylene,*** glycol ethers***
Lacquer thinner	Acetone,** methyl ethyl ketone,** isopropanol,** glycol ethers,*** toluene***
Rubbing oils (Danish oil, antique oil)	VM&P naphtha,* turpentine,** toluene***
Drying oils (boiled linseed oil, polymerized tung oil)	Mineral spirits,* turpentine**
Varnishes (tung oil varnish, spar varnish, varnish stain)	Mineral spirits,* VM&P naphtha*
Polyurethanes (poly varnish, urethane stains)	Mineral spirits,* toluene***
Lacquer/varnish removers	Acetone,** xylene,*** methanol,*** methyl isobutyl ketone,*** toluene***
Waxes (paste wax, furniture wax)	Petroleum naphtha,* turpentine**
	* Safest product ** Mildly hazardous product *** Product to be avoided if possible

TOXIC WOODS

As anyone who has suffered through an allergic or irritating reaction to wood dust will testify, working with certain woods can pose serious health risks. The dust from many species, like black cherry, Douglas-fir, and pine, is known to cause respiratory ailments such as rhinitis (or nasal inflammation) and asthma. Other woods, including oak, ash, and birch, can irritate the skin and eyes.

Some species, like ebony, South American mahogany, and Western red cedar, contain toxic chemicals that can be inhaled, ingested, or absorbed through cuts and scratches. Although the chemicals are present in minute quantities, they may cause problems ranging from headaches to irregular heartbeat. Protect yourself from direct exposure to wood dust by keeping your shop clean and well ventilated. Wear a dust mask for cutting operations. When handling a species which you know or suspect may trigger an allergic reaction, spread a barrier cream on your skin or wear protective gear, including gloves, safety glasses, and long sleeves and pants. Refer to the back endpaper for a chart listing a variety of toxic woods and their possible health effects.

FIRE SAFETY

Considering the number of flammable materials and potential ignition sources in a woodworking shop, fire prevention should be one of your foremost safety concerns. Sawdust, wood, paint, and thinners tend to accumulate; often they are near tools that produce sparks and heat. The combination can prove volatile: When vaporized in a small enough concentration of air, a small quantity of lacquer thinner, for example, can be ignited by a spark from a tool and cause a life-threatening explosion.

The first step in fire safety is prevention. All finishing products and solvents, for example, should be stored away from heat sources in airtight glass or metal containers, preferably in a fireproof cabinet *(page 89)*. Hang rags soaked with flammable chemicals to dry outdoors, or soak them in water and store them in sealed metal containers. When working with finishing products, keep windows open and the shop well ventilated.

Be prepared to deal with a fire effectively. Install a smoke detector on the shop ceiling or a wall, and keep an ABC fire extinguisher nearby. Design a fire evacuation plan that maps out two possible escape routes from each room of the building in which the shop is located. If the fire involves an electric tool, a power cord, or an electrical outlet, shut off the power. Call the fire department immediately, inform them of the nature of the fire, and try to extinguish the blaze yourself. But if the flames cannot be contained, or the fire is coming from inside a wall or ceiling, evacuate the building.

PREPARING AGAINST FIRE

Installing a smoke detector
Open the cover of the detector, hold the base on the ceiling or wall, and mark the screw holes. Bore a hole for a screw anchor at each mark. Tap the anchors into the holes and, holding the detector in position, drive a screw into each anchor to secure the base *(right)*. Install a battery and close the detector cover. Test the device once every month. First, press the test button. Then, blow out a lit match or candle below a vent, letting smoke enter it. Replace the battery if the alarm does not sound for both tests—or if it emits a chirping sound, indicating the battery is weak.

Lock pin

Controlling a fire
To extinguish a small, contained fire, use an ABC-rated dry-chemical fire extinguisher, which is effective against all three major classes of fires: burning wood or other combustibles (Class A), oil- or grease-fed flames (Class B), and electrical blazes (Class C). Position yourself a safe distance from the fire with your back to the nearest exit. Holding the extinguisher upright, pull the lock pin out of the handle *(inset)* and aim the nozzle at the base of the flames. Squeeze the handle and spray in a quick, side-to-side motion *(left)* until the fire is out. Watch for "flashback," or rekindling, and be prepared to spray again. If the fire spreads, leave the building. Dispose of burned waste following the advice of the fire department. After use, have the extinguisher professionally recharged; replace it if it is non-rechargeable.

ELECTRICAL SAFETY

Electricity plays a major role in the modern woodworking shop, powering machines and tools, lighting fixtures and lamps, and heating systems. Electricity is so commonplace that it is all too easy to forget its potential for danger. An electrical shock, even one that can hardly be felt, can be deadly. For this reason, the electrical system is strictly regulated by codes and standards designed to protect you from fire and shock.

Living safely with electricity also requires following basic precautions designed to prevent mishaps. Inspect plugs for cracks and power cords for fraying, and replace any worn or damaged part before using a tool. Never replace a blown fuse with one of a higher amperage. Do not plug a three-prong plug into a two-slot outlet by removing the grounding prong from a three-prong plug. Instead, replace the outlet with a GFCI (right).

Before undertaking a repair, shut off the power at the service panel. To work on the system, wear rubber gloves and, where possible, use only one hand, keeping your free hand behind your back.

PLUGGING IN SAFELY

GFCI outlet

Using GFCI outlets
The U.S. National Electrical Code requires that any new outlet in a garage or unfinished basement must be protected by a ground-fault circuit interrupter (GFCI). A GFCI protects a circuit—and you—by monitoring the flow of electricity passing through it and tripping instantly when it detects a leak to ground. If you need to replace an outlet in your shop, install a GFCI, such as the one shown above, following the manufacturer's directions, or have a qualified electrician do the work. Test the outlet once every month by pushing the TEST button; the RESET button should pop out. If it does not, have the outlet serviced. To reactivate the outlet, press the RESET button.

MINIMUM WIRE GAUGE FOR EXTENSION CORDS

AMPERAGE RATING OF TOOL	MINIMUM GAUGE FOR DIFFERENT LENGTH CORDS		
	25'	50'	75'
0-2.0	18	18	18
2.1-3.4	18	18	18
3.5-5.0	18	18	16
5.1-7.0	18	16	14
7.1-12.0	18	14	12
12.1-16.0	16	12	10

Choosing a wire with the proper gauge
Using an extension cord with the wrong gauge can cause a drop in line voltage, resulting in loss of power, excessive heat, and tool burnout. Refer to the chart at left to determine the minimum wire gauge for the tool and task at hand. If, for instance, your tool has a 7-amp motor and you are using a 75-foot extension cord, the minimum gauge should be 14. Choose only round-jacketed extension cords listed by Underwriters Laboratory (UL).

PERSONAL SAFETY GEAR

The personal safety equipment shown below can go a long way toward shielding you from most dangers in the workshop. But carrying an inventory of safety gear is not enough; the items must be properly used to protect you from injury.

The need for some items may not be readily apparent, although the dangers are very real. Few woodworkers need to be reminded of the cutting power of a spinning saw blade or jointer cutterhead. Less well known are the long-term effects of being exposed to the sound generated by power tools. The chart on the next page lists a variety of power tools along with their approximate noise levels in decibels. The chart also indicates the longest recommended time that an unprotected person can be exposed to various levels before risking permanent hearing loss.

Remember, too, that even short-term exposure to some noise, while it may not lead to hearing loss, can dull the senses and cause a woodworker's alertness to flag—a setup for an accident.

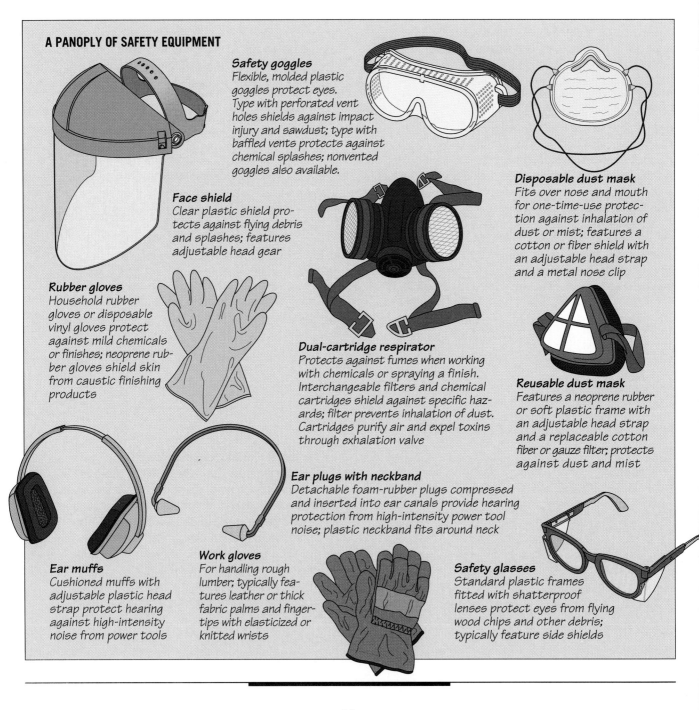

A PANOPLY OF SAFETY EQUIPMENT

Safety goggles
Flexible, molded plastic goggles protect eyes. Type with perforated vent holes shields against impact injury and sawdust; type with baffled vents protects against chemical splashes; nonvented goggles also available.

Face shield
Clear plastic shield protects against flying debris and splashes; features adjustable head gear

Rubber gloves
Household rubber gloves or disposable vinyl gloves protect against mild chemicals or finishes; neoprene rubber gloves shield skin from caustic finishing products

Disposable dust mask
Fits over nose and mouth for one-time-use protection against inhalation of dust or mist; features a cotton or fiber shield with an adjustable head strap and a metal nose clip

Dual-cartridge respirator
Protects against fumes when working with chemicals or spraying a finish. Interchangeable filters and chemical cartridges shield against specific hazards; filter prevents inhalation of dust. Cartridges purify air and expel toxins through exhalation valve

Reusable dust mask
Features a neoprene rubber or soft plastic frame with an adjustable head strap and a replaceable cotton fiber or gauze filter; protects against dust and mist

Ear plugs with neckband
Detachable foam-rubber plugs compressed and inserted into ear canals provide hearing protection from high-intensity power tool noise; plastic neckband fits around neck

Ear muffs
Cushioned muffs with adjustable plastic head strap protect hearing against high-intensity noise from power tools

Work gloves
For handling rough lumber; typically features leather or thick fabric palms and fingertips with elasticized or knitted wrists

Safety glasses
Standard plastic frames fitted with shatterproof lenses protect eyes from flying wood chips and other debris; typically feature side shields

NOISE LEVELS PRODUCED BY POWER TOOLS

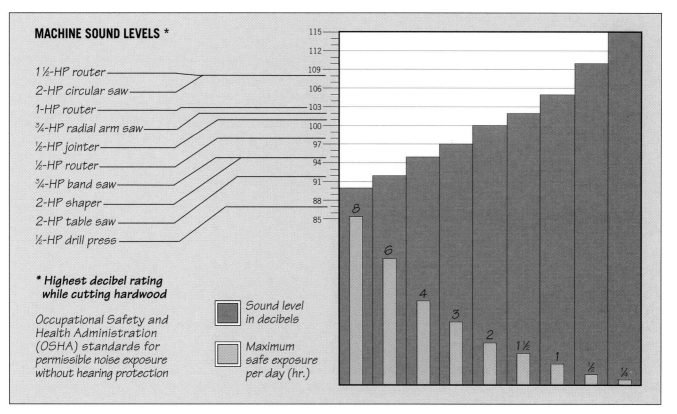

MACHINE SOUND LEVELS *

1½-HP router — 109
2-HP circular saw — 106
1-HP router — 103
¾-HP radial arm saw — 100
½-HP jointer — 97
½-HP router — 94
¾-HP band saw — 91
2-HP shaper — 88
2-HP table saw — 85
½-HP drill press —

***Highest decibel rating while cutting hardwood**

Occupational Safety and Health Administration (OSHA) standards for permissible noise exposure without hearing protection

Sound level in decibels

Maximum safe exposure per day (hr.)

(Chart values: 8, 6, 4, 3, 2, 1½, 1, ½, ¼)

While a ½-horsepower drill press is unlikely to damage your hearing—unless you run the machine all day long—unprotected exposure to the noise produced by a 1 ½-horsepower router can be dangerous after only 30 minutes. The above chart shows approximate noise levels produced by a variety of power tools. Keep in mind that tools with dull cutters or blades generate more noise than those with well-sharpened cutting edges.

TESTING A RESPIRATOR

Checking for air leaks

A respirator is only as good as its seal against your face. No seal, no protection. To test your respirator, place it over your face, setting the top strap over the crown of your head. Adjust the side straps for a snug fit. To test the respirator, cover the outlet valve with your hand and breathe out gently *(right)*. There should be no air leakage around the facepiece. If air leaks out of the respirator, readjust the straps for a tighter fit. Replace the facepiece when necessary following the manufacturer's instructions, or replace the respirator. Use the appropriate filters for the job at hand. (If you have a beard, use a full-face mask with forced-air ventilation.)

BUILD IT YOURSELF

A VARIETY OF PUSH STICK DESIGNS

12"

14"

45°

Notch

12"

PUSH STICKS

Push sticks for feeding stock across stationary tool tables can be purchased ready-made, but they are easy to make in the shop using ¾-inch plywood scraps and a band saw or saber saw. The variations shown above can serve as rough guides, but no one shape is ideal for every situation. Design a push stick that is comfortable to hold and suited to the machine and operation at hand. The long base of a rectangular push stick *(above, left)* or shoe-shaped model *(above, right)* allows you to apply firm downward pressure on a workpiece. Either design will effectively keep your hands away from a blade or cutter while pushing narrow stock across a saw table.

For most cuts on a table saw, design a push stick with a 45° angle between the handle and the base *(above, center)*. A push stick featuring a smaller angle, with the handle closer to the table, works better for ripping wood

on a radial arm saw. Whatever design you choose, the notch on the bottom edge must be deep enough to support the workpiece, but shallow enough not to contact the machine table. You can also chamfer the edges of the handle for a more comfortable grip.

Keep your push sticks close at hand, ready to feed stock when necessary.

To use a push stick on a radial arm saw *(below)*, set it against the trailing end of the workpiece and feed it into the blade; at the same time, apply some side pressure to keep the stock flush against the fence. When the cut is completed, retract the push stick carefully to prevent it from catching in the blade.

PUSH BLOCK

Handle
³/₄" x 2 ¹/₂" x 12"

Base
³/₄" x 3 ¹/₂" x 15"

Lip
³/₈" x ³/₄" x 3 ¹/₂"

A PUSH BLOCK FOR FACE JOINTING

The long, wide base of the push block shown above is ideal for surfacing the face of a board on a jointer. Although push blocks for such jobs are available commercially, you can easily fashion your own. Refer to the illustration for suggested dimensions, but tailor the design to suit your own needs.

Cut the pieces to size, then glue the lip to the underside of the base, flush with one end. Screw the handle to the top, positioning it so the back is even with the end of the base. Drive the screws from the underside of the base; be sure to countersink the fasteners to avoid marring the workpiece when you feed it across the jointer knives. Bore a hole near the front end of the base so you can hang the push block on the wall when it is not in use.

To use the push block, set the work-piece on the jointer's infeed table a few inches from the knives, butting its edge against the fence. Then lay the push block squarely on top of the stock, centered between its sides, with the lip over the trailing end of the workpiece. With your leading hand on the front end of the stock and your thumb braced against the push block, slowly feed the workpiece across the knives *(left)*. (For stock thinner than ¾ inch, use only the push block.) Apply downward pressure to keep the stock flat on the tables and lateral pressure to keep it butted against the fence.

Fence

Infeed table

BUILD IT YOURSELF (continued)

FEATHERBOARDS

Featherboards, also known as fingerboards, are used to keep stock pressed snugly against the fence or table of a stationary tool. They also serve as anti-kickback devices, since the fingers allow a workpiece to move in only one direction—toward the blade or bit. Two basic designs are shown at right. The miter-slot featherboard is attached to a bar that is clamped in the miter slot of a woodworking machine table. The standard featherboard is clamped directly to the table or fence.

To make either type, cut a ¾-inch-thick board 3 to 4 inches wide and long enough to suit the job at hand. Cut a 30°- to 45°- miter at the end of the board, then mark a parallel line about 5 inches from the mitered end. Cut a series of ⅛-inch-wide slots to the marked line about ⅛ inch apart, creating a row of pliable fingers. For

FEATHERBOARDS

Notch

Standard featherboard

Fingers and slots

Miter-slot featherboard

Miter bar

the miter-slot type, rout a slot down the middle of the board wide enough for a machine screw; also cut a wood bar the length and width of the table's miter slot. Bore a hole for the screw through the bar, countersinking it so the screw head can be recessed in

the underside of the bar. (A carriage bolt or flat-head machine screw will work well.) To set up the featherboard, slip the screw through the bar, fit the bar in the table miter slot, and use a washer and wing nut to fasten the featherboard tightly to the bar so its fingers hold the workpiece against the fence. Clamp the miter bar in place at the front or back of the table.

For the standard featherboard, cut a notch out of one edge to accommodate a support board. To use the device on the table saw *(left)*, clamp one featherboard to the fence above the blade, and place a second one halfway between the blade and the front of the table. Clamp a support board perpendicular to the featherboard for extra pressure to prevent it from creeping out of place. For the cut shown, feed the workpiece into the blade until your trailing fingers reach the featherboards. Then, with the saw still running, move to the back of the table and pull the workpiece past the blade. Or, use a push stick to complete the cut.

Fence

Support board

FIRST AID

Most woodworking accidents arise from the improper use of tools and safety guards, unsafe work habits, and mishandling hazardous materials. Take the time to set up properly for a job, gathering together the tools, equipment, and materials you need. Always use the appropriate safety gear. Work methodically; never hurry through a job.

Be especially careful—or stop working—if you are fatigued.

Accidents can befall even the most careful woodworker. Boards split, blades nick, and liquids splash. Many finishing products contain chemicals that emit toxic fumes, causing dizziness or nausea. Keep in mind the potential hazards of any tool or material you use. Store a

first-aid kit, stocked with the basic supplies shown below, in an easily accessible spot in your shop. In the event of an accident, you will want anyone to be able to find it quickly to administer first aid. Keep emergency telephone numbers handy. Techniques for handling some common shop mishaps are shown on the following pages.

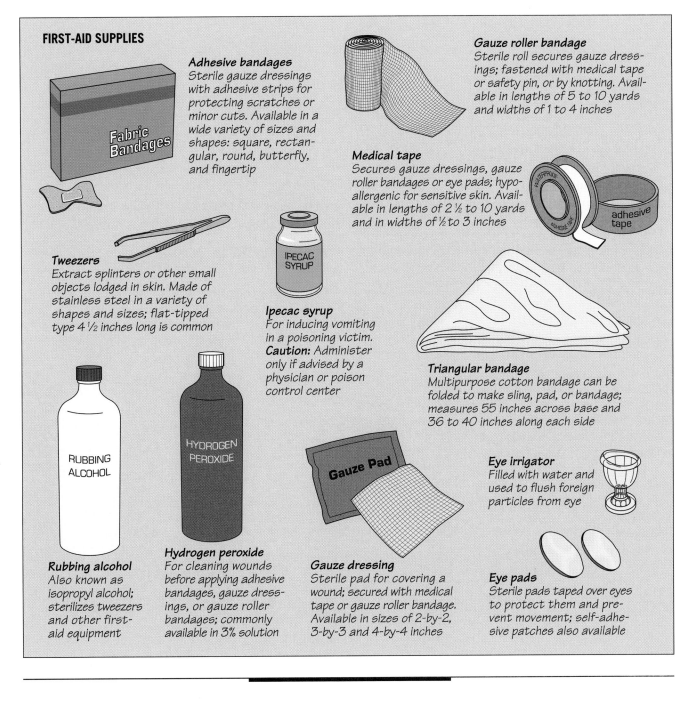

FIRST-AID SUPPLIES

Adhesive bandages
Sterile gauze dressings with adhesive strips for protecting scratches or minor cuts. Available in a wide variety of sizes and shapes: square, rectangular, round, butterfly, and fingertip

Gauze roller bandage
Sterile roll secures gauze dressings; fastened with medical tape or safety pin, or by knotting. Available in lengths of 5 to 10 yards and widths of 1 to 4 inches

Medical tape
Secures gauze dressings, gauze roller bandages or eye pads; hypoallergenic for sensitive skin. Available in lengths of 2 ½ to 10 yards and in widths of ½ to 3 inches

Tweezers
Extract splinters or other small objects lodged in skin. Made of stainless steel in a variety of shapes and sizes; flat-tipped type 4 ½ inches long is common

Ipecac syrup
For inducing vomiting in a poisoning victim. **Caution:** Administer only if advised by a physician or poison control center

Triangular bandage
Multipurpose cotton bandage can be folded to make sling, pad, or bandage; measures 55 inches across base and 36 to 40 inches along each side

Eye irrigator
Filled with water and used to flush foreign particles from eye

Rubbing alcohol
Also known as isopropyl alcohol; sterilizes tweezers and other first-aid equipment

Hydrogen peroxide
For cleaning wounds before applying adhesive bandages, gauze dressings, or gauze roller bandages; commonly available in 3% solution

Gauze dressing
Sterile pad for covering a wound; secured with medical tape or gauze roller bandage. Available in sizes of 2-by-2, 3-by-3 and 4-by-4 inches

Eye pads
Sterile pads taped over eyes to protect them and prevent movement; self-adhesive patches also available

PROVIDING MINOR FIRST AID

Eye irrigator

Clearing a particle from the eye

Hold your affected eye open with the forefinger and thumb of one hand. Slowly rotate your eye, if necessary, to help expose the particle. Gently wipe away the particle using the twisted end of a tissue moistened with water *(above, left)*. Or, fill an eye irrigator with cool water and use it to flush out the particle. Lean forward with both eyes closed and press the rim of the irrigator against the affected eye, and tilt back your head. Open your eyes *(above, right)* and blink several times to flush out the particle. If you cannot remove the particle, seek medical help immediately. **Caution:** Do not remove a particle that is on the cornea, is embedded, or has adhered to the eye.

Flushing a chemical from the eye

Holding the eyelids of the affected eye apart, flush the eye thoroughly for at least 15 minutes under a gentle flow of cool water from a faucet *(right)* or pitcher; tilt your head to one side to prevent the chemical from being washed into the uninjured eye. If you are outdoors, flush the eye using a garden hose. Gently cover both eyes with eye pads or sterile gauze dressings and seek medical help immediately.

Pulling out a splinter

Wash the skin around the splinter with soap and water. (A metal splinter, even if you are able to remove it, may require treatment for tetanus; seek medical help.) To remove the splinter, sterilize a needle and tweezers with rubbing alcohol. Ease the end of the splinter out from under the skin using the needle, then pull it out with the tweezers *(right)*. Clean the skin again with soap and water. If the splinter cannot be removed, seek medical attention.

Tweezers

Treating a cut

Wrap the wound in a clean cloth and apply direct pressure with your hand to stop any bleeding; keep the wound elevated. If the cloth becomes blood-soaked, wrap another cloth over it. If bleeding persists or the wound is deep or gaping, seek medical help. Otherwise, wash the wound with soap and water, then bandage it; for a narrow, shallow wound, draw its edges closed with a butterfly bandage *(left)*.

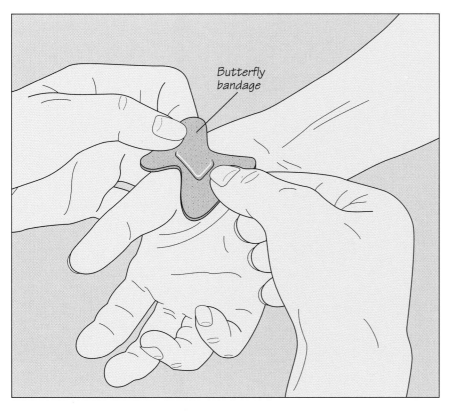

Butterfly bandage

CONTROLLING BLEEDING

Applying direct pressure to stop bleeding
To help stop profuse or rapid bleeding, apply direct pressure to the wound with a gauze dressing or a clean cloth and, if possible, elevate the injury *(above, left)*. Direct pressure should stop the flow of blood and allow it to clot. If the dressing becomes blood-soaked, add another over the first one; avoid lifting the dressing to inspect the wound. It will be easier to maintain steady pressure if you wrap the wound with a roller bandage *(above, right)* for added direct pressure. If you cannot stop the bleeding, call for medical help.

HANDLING A SHOCK VICTIM

Treating a shock victim
Some degree of shock—either immediate or delayed—accompanies any injury. Shock can be provoked by loss of blood, pain, or an allergic reaction. Signs of shock include anxiety or confusion; cold or clammy skin; weak, irregular breathing or pulse; and loss of consciousness. If you suspect an injury victim is suffering from shock, immediately call for emergency help. If the victim is conscious, place him on his back with his feet propped up 8 to 12 inches above the level of his head *(right)*. Loosen the victim's clothing around the neck, chest, and waist. Keep the victim warm with a blanket, but avoid overheating. Do not give the victim anything to eat or drink.

TREATING A VICTIM OF ELECTRICAL SHOCK

Freeing a victim from a live current

A person who contacts a live current may experience only a mild tingling sensation. Sometimes, however, the victim's muscles contract involuntarily around the source. Do not touch the victim or the electrical source. Instead, immediately stop the flow of electricity in the circuit at a wall switch or the service panel. If the electricity cannot be shut off immediately, use a dry wood implement, such as a broom handle, to knock the victim free of the electrical source *(right)*. Call for medical help immediately, then check the victim's breathing and pulse. If there is no breathing, give mouth-to-mouth resuscitation; if there is no pulse, give cardiopulmonary resuscitation (CPR) only if you are qualified. If the victim is breathing and has no neck or back injury, place him in the recovery position *(below)*. Tilt the victim's head back face to draw his tongue away from his throat and keep the airway open. Keep the victim calm until help arrives.

SHOP LAYOUT

Even in spacious shops, tools occasionally need to be moved around; in small shops, reassigning floor space may be a part of every project. A wheeled base can make a 10-inch table saw, like the one pictured here, easy to reposition.

As they gain experience and accumulate tools, most woodworkers pine for their own special place to practice their skills. In their fantasies, the workshop is an airy space equipped with a substantial workbench and an array of stationary machines and portable tools. The reality for many woodworkers, however, is much more modest. The typical shop never seems to have enough light, power, or elbow room.

Few homes have space specifically designed as a workshop area. As a result, setting up a home shop demands creativity and flexibility; the task often involves converting an area originally intended for some other purpose. With careful planning and forethought, however, a location that might appear unsuitable can be turned into an efficient, comfortable place to work.

Although size is often the first consideration, several other concerns may be more important. For example, situating a shop in a spare room on the main floor of a home may provide a large working area, but noise and dust from tools would probably inconvenience other members of the family. To suit their own needs without intruding too much on the people they live with, woodworkers commonly locate home shops in the basement or a garage. Each has its pros and cons. A basement is apt to be damp and may need to have its wiring and heating upgraded; access can be hampered by narrow doors, tight stairways, and low ceilings; and ventilation may be inadequate for finishing tasks. A garage, on the other hand, is apt to be cold; it may require wiring and heating. The woodworker may end up jostling for space with a car or two.

Still, with a bit of planning and the proper layout, even these locations can be turned to your advantage: A basement can be heated and powered more easily than a garage. On the other hand, a garage has a larger door through which to move lumber and sheet materials like plywood, its air is less humid, and the din of power tools and fumes of finishing can be isolated from living spaces.

This chapter outlines some basic principles to follow when designing a new shop or upgrading an existing one. Topics include planning *(pages 30 and 31)*; allowing adequate space for tools *(pages 32-40)*; and providing for necessities like heat, light, and electrical power *(pages 41-45)*. By listing your objectives and closely examining your work, you can apply these principles to create a layout that suits your own needs.

Every hour spent planning shop layout pays dividends later on. To determine the best way to arrange the tools planned for the shop, a woodworker places overhead-view silhouettes of the tools on a scale drawing of the space.

WORKSHOP PLANNING

I t is far easier to shuffle paper cutouts of your tools on a template than it is to drag a table saw halfway across the shop. Time spent planning the layout of your shop will be more than amply rewarded in reduced frustration and increased efficiency when you go to work.

Designing a shop involves juggling many interdependent variables, from local humidity and the type of work you do to the height of the ceiling and the cost of wiring. To help sort them out, ask yourself a set of questions, like those in the checklist on page 31, to help determine the kind of shop most suitable for your needs and remind you of factors that may affect its design. Remember, too, a basic principle for

any shop, illustrated below, that the lumber should take a relatively straight path as it is processed—almost as though the shop were an assembly line.

A multipurpose stationary power tool can help you make the most of a cramped workspace. The machine at right is an all-in-one table saw, drill press, disk sander, and lathe. Accessory attachments also allow it to serve as a band saw, jigsaw, and jointer.

Refer to the illustrated inventory of stationary machines and tables starting on page 32 as a guide to space and lighting requirements. The best way to design

TOOL PLACEMENT AND WORK FLOW

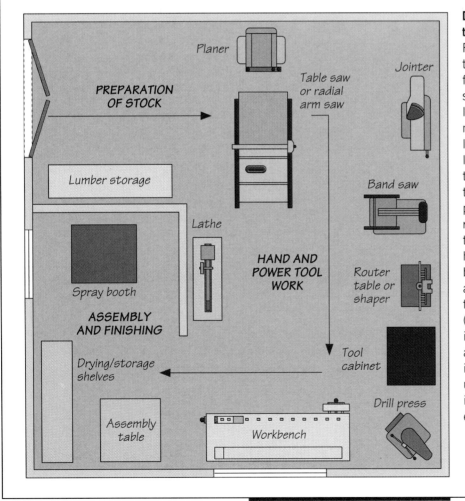

Planer

Table saw or radial arm saw

Jointer

PREPARATION OF STOCK

Lumber storage

Lathe

Band saw

HAND AND POWER TOOL WORK

Router table or shaper

Spray booth

ASSEMBLY AND FINISHING

Drying/storage shelves

Tool cabinet

Drill press

Assembly table

Workbench

Designing a shop around the woodworking process

For maximum efficiency, lay out the tools in your shop so that the lumber follows a fairly direct route from rough stock to finished pieces. The diagram at left illustrates a logical work flow for a medium-size workshop. At the upper left-hand corner is the entrance where lumber is stored on racks. To the right is the stock preparation area, devoted to the table saw (or radial arm saw), jointer, and planer; at this station, lumber is cut to rough length and surfaced. The heart of the next work area, near the bottom right-hand corner of the drawing, is the workbench. Radiating outward from the bench are the shop's other stationary tools—in this case, a drill press, lathe, router table (or shaper), and band saw. A tool cabinet is nearby. Moving clockwise, the final work area is set aside for assembly and finishing. This station features a table for gluing up pieces and shelves for drying and storing. The spray booth is close by, but isolated from the shop by walls on three sides.

the layout is to experiment with arranging photocopies of scale drawings of the tools (page 35) on a sheet of graph paper. Remember that a tool should be positioned so that an access door is visible from it. In addition, a workpiece kicked back from the tool should not be able to strike someone working at another station.

Consider dedicating spaces for specific woodworking tasks. A finishing area or spray booth requires priority in planning because of light, temperature, and ventilation needs.

Depending on the extent of your shop and local zoning and building codes, you may need to obtain permits; consult your local building inspection office.

SHOP TIP

A table saw on wheels

Because it is the largest and heaviest woodworking tool in many shops, a table saw usually stays put, which can be a drawback in a small shop where space is at a premium. By mounting it on wheels, however, you can easily shift your saw out of the way when it is not in use. If your saw did not come with a wheeled base, measure the base of the motor housing and have a metalworking shop build a rolling base to your specifications. For maximum maneuverability, the base should have three wheels, including one that pivots. Keep the saw from moving or tipping when it is in use by wedging two triangular wood shims under the wheels at the front of the base.

A SHOP LAYOUT CHECKLIST

LOCATION

• Which available areas in and around your home are appropriate for a shop?

• How easy is the access to these areas?

• Is the electric wiring adequate for powering your tools and lighting?

• How well are the areas heated, insulated, and ventilated?

• Will shop noise disturb other areas?

• If the location is a basement, will the shop be sharing space with a furnace room or laundry room?

• If the location is an outbuilding or garage, how much space is taken up by cars, bicycles, lawn mowers, and so on?

• Does the building or garage have any heating, electricity, or plumbing?

• How secure is the building or garage from theft?

TYPE OF WORK

• What type of woodworking projects will you be doing?

• What size are the materials you will need to move in and out of the shop?

• How much space will be devoted to storing lumber and work-in-progress?

• What stationary machines, portable power tools, and hand tools will you need?

• Are there enough electrical circuits to supply your power needs?

• How many lighting fixtures does your work require?

• How many workbenches, assembly tables, and accessories like tool cabinets, scrap bins, and sawhorses will you need?

• Will local seasonal temperatures and humidity affect your work?

• Will you be doing a lot of finishing work?

WORK HABITS

• What room temperature will you need to work comfortably?

• What type of light do you prefer for working?

• Will you be working during daylight hours, or will you be using the shop at night?

• Which tools do you expect to use most often?

• Will you be working alone in the shop, or will it be used by another worker? Would that person have easy access to the shop?

• Will you need to lock the shop or keep it off-limits to children or pets?

• How many hours per day do you expect to spend in the shop?

• Is the flooring made of a material that is comfortable to stand on for long periods of time?

PLANNING FOR STATIONARY TOOLS

TABLE SAW

LIGHTING
Needs light from above, to the left of and behind blade

CLEARANCE
Needs enough clearance around table for long boards; keep line of work clear. Best location is center of shop

BAND SAW

LIGHTING
Needs light from above and to the right of blade; portable clamp-on light can be used

CLEARANCE
No clearance needed on throat-column side; requires 4 feet of clearance on other sides for long boards. Keep line of work clear. Can be positioned against a wall or in a corner

RADIAL ARM SAW

LIGHTING
Needs light from sides, front and above

CLEARANCE
No clearance needed behind tool; good location is against wall. Allow about 12 feet of clearance on either side for long boards

ROUTER TABLE

LIGHTING
Needs light from front and both sides

CLEARANCE
Relatively portable. Allow at least 6 feet of clearance in front and to the sides when in operation; needs no clearance behind table. Good location is against wall; keep line of work clear so that a kicked back workpiece would not strike another worker

DRILL PRESS

LIGHTING
Light must focus directly on bit from overhead; portable clamp-on light can be used

CLEARANCE
No clearance needed behind tool; good location is against wall. Allow 3 feet of clearance on either side, and enough clearance in front for wide work

SHAPER

LIGHTING
Needs light from front and sides

CLEARANCE
Allow at least 6 feet of clearance in front and to the sides; no clearance needed behind tool. Good location is against wall; keep line of work clear so that a workpiece that is kicked back will not strike another worker

JOINTER/PLANER

LIGHTING
Needs light from above and front of tables

CLEARANCE
Allow 3 to 4 feet of clearance on sides, more for long boards; keep line of work clear. Good location is near lumber storage rack for easy surfacing of stock

JOINTER

LIGHTING
Needs light from left and rear of tool

CLEARANCE
Allow 3 feet of clearance in front of tables and enough clearance on both sides for long boards; keep line of work clear. Best location is behind or to left of table saw

LATHE

LIGHTING
Overhead light must focus directly on work

CLEARANCE
Leave 3 feet of clearance in front; can be positioned against a wall since work is contained by tool

BENCH GRINDER

Best location is near lathe since the cutting tools used with it require frequent grinding. Needs clearance and light on front only; portable clamp-on light can be aimed directly at wheel

ASSEMBLY AND FINISHING TABLE

LIGHTING
Needs light from above and sides; natural light preferable

CLEARANCE
Minimal clearance needed; good location is near window

STATIONARY BELT SANDER

LIGHTING
Needs light from front and left of tool

CLEARANCE
Allow 5 to 6 feet of clearance to the sides for long work; leave 3 to 4 feet in front of and to either side of disk sander. Keep line of work clear

SCROLL SAW

LIGHTING
Light needed to the right of blade; portable clamp-on light can be used to shine directly on work

CLEARANCE
Needs 5 feet of clearance at front and sides; no clearance needed behind tool. Good location is against wall

WORKBENCH

LIGHTING
Needs light from above, particularly over vises

CLEARANCE
Allow 3 feet of clearance around vises; can be placed against wall if necessary

SCALE DRAWINGS OF STATIONARY TOOLS

Band saw

Belt sander

Drill press

Jointer

Lathe

Radial arm saw

Scroll saw

Shaper

Table saw

Assembly table

Dust collector

Jointer/Planer

Lumber rack

Workbench

Router table

Grinder

Tool storage

Laying out a workshop on paper

The illustrations above are overhead views of a dozen typical stationary tools drawn at a scale of ¼ inch to 1 foot. To facilitate the task of arranging your tools on the shop floor, sketch your workshop space on a sheet of similarly scaled graph paper. Then photocopy this page, cut out the tools you need, and arrange the cutouts on the grid to determine the best layout for your shop. Consider the space and light requirements of the tools *(pages 32-34)* when assigning space to each one. Also factor in your shop's electrical and lighting needs *(pages 41-43)*. Use the sample layouts of a small-, medium-, and large-size shop beginning on page 36 as guidelines to get you started.

LAYOUT OF A SMALL SHOP

Laying out the shop

The illustration below shows one way of making efficient use of the space in a small shop—in this case, one-half of a two-car garage. The three stationary machines chosen are essential for most projects: the table saw, the jointer, and the band saw. The saw and jointer are mounted on casters so they can be moved if necessary. With the bench and table there is ample space for hand tool and portable power tool work. The storage space— perforated hardboard and shelving—is located along the walls; a lumber rack is positioned near the garage door. Any exposed

framing in the ceiling could also be used to hold stock. Refer to the key in the bottom right-hand corner of the illustration for the type and location of electrical outlets and light fixtures. Note that there is an overhead master switch (near the bench's tail vise) that controls all three machines. Attention is also paid to feed direction of each machine (represented by the arrowhead in the key); the access door to the shop is always in the user's field of vision. **Caution:** If your shop shares space with motorized equipment you will not be able to spray finishes.

Workbench

Scrap
bin

Short
stock storage

Shelving

Table saw

Work table

Perforated hard-
board wall storage

Band saw

Sawhorses

Jointer

Lumber
rack

11'

22'

KEY

⏚ 240 V outlet
⏛ 120 V outlet
◉ Incandescent light fixture
⊙⊙ Fluorescent light fixture
◼ Overhead switch for power tools
▲ Direction of feed

SHOP TIP

A safe attention-getter
If the door to the shop is outside your field of vision when you are at a machine, there is the risk that someone might enter the shop, tap you on the shoulder, and startle you. To avoid accident-causing surprises, mount a light bulb at eye level near the tool and wire the switch to the door frame so that the bulb lights when the door is opened. Wiring another bulb to the bell circuit of the telephone can solve the problem of missing phone calls: Each time the bell rings, the bulb will light.

BUILD IT YOURSELF

A SHOP DOLLY

To wheel workpieces or large projects around the shop, use the shop-built dolly shown below. Start with the base and corner blocks, cutting them from ¾-inch plywood to a size that suits your needs. Screw the corner blocks in place, then fasten

Corner block

Top

Shelf

Skirt

Leg

Base

a caster onto each block *(above)*. To build the shelved section, cut the skirts and the eight pieces for the legs from 1-by-3 stock; the shelf from ½-inch plywood; and the top from ¾-inch plywood. The legs should be long enough for the top to sit at a comfortable height. Screw the leg pieces together, then attach the skirts to the legs' inside faces. Fasten the shelf and the top to the skirts. Secure the legs to the base with angle brackets.

SAVING SPACE

Setting up a shop in the attic

Attic shops have several strikes against them: They are often uninsulated and their floors are not designed to support heavy weight. In addition, headroom is limited and access can present problems, especially if you are working with long planks or full sheets of plywood. But for a luthier, carver, or woodworker who specializes in small projects, an attic can be an ideal spot for a shop. As shown in the illustration at left, nailing sheets of sheathing-grade plywood to the joists will produce a floor that is sufficiently sturdy to hold up a workbench and one of the lighter stationary machines, like the band saw. The spaces between the studs and rafters and down near the eaves—where the roof and attic floor meet—are ideal for storing lumber, tools, and supplies.

Positioning stationary machines in a confined space

If your workshop is cramped you may have to forego an ideal placement of stationary machines to allow you to make the most of your limited space. Consider the design of your machines and the feed direction you need to use; you may be able to place two machines close together if they are matched properly. The high table of a band saw and the feed direction normally used with the machine, for example, makes it an ideal match in a tight space with a jointer *(right)*. The two can be placed close together while still providing adequate space to operate each machine at separate times.

LAYOUT OF A MEDIUM-SIZE SHOP

Setting up a basement shop

The medium-size shop represented below shares many of the features of the small shop *(page 36)*: the table saw and jointer-planer are on casters; a master switch (this time near the door) controls all the machines; the machines are positioned so users will see the door near the bench; perforated hardboard and shelves for storage line the perimeter of the shop (supplies can also be stored under the stairs); and the lumber

rack is located near the main access door at the foot of the stairs. With the extra space, this shop has room for a lathe, a drill press, and a dust collector. A work table for glue-up and finishing is positioned at a window with an exhaust fan. The focal point of this shop is the table saw; it is equidistant from the stock preparation area in front of it, the workbench to one side, and the work table behind it.

KEY
⌀ *240 V outlet*
⌀ *120 V outlet*
◉ *Incandescent light fixture*
⊙ *Fluorescent light fixture*
▣ *Overhead switch for power tools*
▲ *Direction of feed*

20'

18'

Shelves

Workbench

Drill press

Perforated hardboard

Dust collector

Stairs

Sawhorses

Jointer/ planer

Stool

Table saw

Lathe

Work table

Shelves

Band saw

Scrap bin

Window fan

Lumber rack

LAYOUT OF A LARGE SHOP

Converting a two-car garage

Setting up a shop with all the features shown below calls for a large space, like a two-car garage. This shop has many of the characteristics of the smaller shops examined earlier, with additional tools and conveniences that allow it to handle a wider range of projects. At one corner is a spacious finishing room, partitioned from the rest of the shop and equipped with an explosion-proof fan to exhaust fumes. The shop includes a bathroom with a sink and a toilet. In addition to the machines featured earlier, this has a radial arm saw, shaper, and planer. The

shop boasts three separate work surfaces: one in the finishing room, one for glue-up near the drill press, and a workbench beside the table saw. A shop of this size would need an independent electrical service panel to power all the tools. To keep the wiring out of the way, half the floor is covered with a raised ¾-inch plywood floor; as shown on page 44, an understructure of 1-by-2s is laid on the concrete floor on 12-inch centers and the plywood is nailed to the boards. Wires are run in conduits under the plywood between the 1-by-2s.

ELECTRICAL POWER

Electric power requirement should be considered early in the process of planning a shop's layout. Allow for growth. Then, as you add new tools and light fixtures, you will avoid the headaches of an inadequate system: repeated tripping of circuit breakers or blowing of fuses, and octopus adapters funneling several power cords into one outlet.

If you plan to wire your shop to your home's main service panel, be sure that your electrical supply has enough additional power. You can get a rough idea of how many amperes your shop will draw from the system by totaling the amperage of all the tools you plan to use and dividing the result in half. If your system is barely able to handle the demands being placed on it by your household, you probably will need to upgrade your service entrance—in other words, increase the number of amps the service panel can draw from the utility company. If the shop will be some distance from the main service panel, it is a good idea to install a 50-amp sub-

panel dedicated to the shop. Another point to remember: Any woodworking machine that draws more than six amps should be on a separate (dedicated) circuit, unless the tool's motor is shielded.

Refer to the illustration on page 42 as a guide to planning the electrical layout of your shop. As you plan, remember that even simple electrical jobs, like extending a circuit or replacing an outlet, can be dangerous. They can also cause a fair amount of damage—ranging from burned-out tool motors to a house fire—if they are carried out improperly. Unless you are qualified and comfortable with the idea of wiring your shop to the electrical system, have a qualified electrician do the job.

The workbench is a natural work surface for using portable power tools. Mounting a power strip on one of the legs and plugging it into an outlet eliminates the need for a separate extension cord for every tool.

ELECTRICAL LAYOUT TIPS

• When planning the electrical layout for your shop, make sure that outlets for power tools and lighting fixtures are on separate circuits.

• Unless your shop has bright windows or your lights are equipped with battery backups, include at least two separate lighting circuits in your electrical layout. In the event one circuit is disabled, the lights plugged into the other circuit will still work.

• Place outlets close to the eventual location of the tools they will power; distribute outlets all around the shop to allow for future tool acquisitions.

• Avoid locating outlets on the floor; they will eventually become filled with sawdust and be a fire hazard.

• Avoid plugging tools into one outlet using an octopus adapter; this can overload your electrical system, and is a sign

that the wiring of your shop is inadequate. Upgrade the system by installing new outlets and wiring them to a separate circuit on the service panel.

• Protect any new outlet in a garage or basement by installing a ground-fault circuit interrupter (GFCI).

• Never work on the wiring of the service panel; entrance wires may remain live even when power is shut off at the main circuit breaker or fuse block.

• Make certain that any new circuits or service sub-panels installed in your home or outbuilding are grounded to the main service panel. Individual outlets must also be grounded.

• Do not take off the cover of the service panel.

• Never work on your wiring in damp or wet conditions.

• Do not touch a metal faucet, pipe, appliance, or other object when working on your wiring.

• Never splice a power cord or an extension cord, or remove the grounding prong from a three-prong plug.

• Use an extension cord to supply electricity to an area only temporarily—not as permanent wiring.

• Never run a power cord or an extension cord under a rug, mat, or carpet; do not fasten the cord using tacks, pins, or staples.

• Never replace a blown fuse with one of higher amperage; do not use a penny, a washer, or foil as a substitute for a fuse.

• If a circuit breaker trips or a fuse blows repeatedly, check for a short circuit, and determine whether the circuit is overloaded.

ELECTRICAL LAYOUT FOR A MEDIUM-SIZE SHOP

Breaker box

Workbench

Drill press
6 amps/120 V

Table saw
12 amps/240 V

Jointer
13.5 amps/240 V

Lathe
9.5 amps/120 V

Band saw
8 amps/120 V

Work table

Lumber rack

KEY

◯ 240 V outlet
◯ 120 V outlet
◉ Incandescent lighting fixture
⊙ Fluorescent lighting fixture
▲ Direction of feed

Wiring the shop

The illustration at left shows one electrical layout for a medium-size shop. The shop has six separate electrical circuits: four for tools and two for lighting. The basic principle to keep in mind is that no circuit using 12-gauge wire should carry more than 80 percent of its capacity; for 20-amp circuits, this means the combined amperage of the tools on the same circuit plus 25 percent of the rating of the largest motor must not exceed 16 amps. In this shop, the table saw and jointer are on separate 240 V circuits; their power cords are suspended from the ceiling with twist-type outlets, which keep the plugs in place. With a combined load of 15 amps, the band saw and the drill press are on the same 120 V circuit; the lathe is on another. Additional outlets on the 120 V circuits can be used for portable tools. The incandescent and fluorescent lighting circuits are separate so that if one fails the other will still work.

SHOP TIP

Power cord covers

Power cords lying loosely on a shop floor are accidents waiting to happen. If your shop does not have overhead outlets for your machines, cover the cords with wood bridges. Cut the covers from 3/4-by-2 1/2 hardwood stock and rout a groove along the length of one face to house the cord. Cut bevels on the opposite face so the cover will not be an obstruction.

LIGHTING

If you find yourself cutting off line or cannot properly examine a finish unless you take your work outside, the lighting in your workshop may need an upgrade. At best, a poorly lit shop will merely bring on fatigue; at worst, it can contribute to sloppy, imprecise work and to accidents.

Fluorescent lights are the most popular type of workshop lighting fixture. They cast a relatively shadowless light, the tubes are long-lasting, and they use 20 percent to 30 percent less electricity than incandescent lights of the same brightness. Many woodworkers find that too much fluorescent light can result in fatigue and headaches, however, and prefer the warmth of incandescent and tungsten lights.

At a minimum, a shop bigger than 120 square feet needs 2 watts of incandescent light or ¾ watt of fluorescent light per square foot. As in the electrical layout illustrated on page 42, shop lights should be circuits separate from

your tools. Ideally, the light fixtures will be divided between two separate circuits. As a rule of thumb, do not exceed 1600 watts on one 20-amp circuit. Also, distribute lighting fixtures around the shop; mounting a single fixture in the middle of the ceiling will make it difficult to illuminate the shadowy areas at the edges of the shop.

If possible, make the most of natural light; there is no better substitute, especially for hand-tool work and finishing. Trying to evaluate planing, sanding, and finishing jobs under artificial light can be frustrating. Both fluorescent and incandescent light tend to distort or disguise the surface texture of natural and finished wood surfaces. Natural light, particularly from the north, has a soft, non-glare quality. If your shop has a window that faces north, place your workbench under it.

Keep in mind that upgrading the lighting in your shop need not entail purchasing expensive fixtures and

rewiring the system. Simply painting a concrete floor a light color or covering the ceiling with white tiles will allow these surfaces to reflect light, rather than absorb it.

A clamp-on lamp can shed all the light you need to work safely at a tool. Mounted on a drill press, this lamp's flexible neck aims a 40-watt bulb directly at the machine's work table.

SHOP TIP

A bench-dog lamp support
For a movable source of light at your workbench, attach a desk lamp to one of the bench dogs. Bore a hole the same diameter as the shaft of the lamp into the head of a wooden dog (page 62). The light can then be positioned at any of the dog holes along the bench.

FLOORS, WALLS, AND CEILINGS

Standing in one place for hours on a concrete floor can strain your feet and legs. An old piece of carpet or a commercial anti-fatigue mat provides a cushion that can be easily moved about the shop.

Since most workshops are set up in basements or garages, concrete floors are a common feature. Yet for anyone who has to spend much time standing on concrete or sweeping it clean, the material can prove both uncomfortable and inconvenient. The hard surface is particularly tough on tools that are dropped accidentally.

Simply painting a concrete floor with a paint made specifically for the purpose will keep down the dust and make the surface easier to clean. Adhesive vinyl floor tile can be laid down as well. Yet many woodworkers prefer the comfort of a raised wooden floor. A simple floor can be constructed from sheets of ¾-inch plywood laid atop a grid of 1-by-2s on 12-inch centers. Not only is this type of floor easier on the feet, but wiring for stationary power tools can be routed underneath the raised surface in ½-inch plastic or steel conduit.

Unlike the walls of most homes, those of separate workshops seldom are insu-lated. If you live in a northern climate, you can increase the thermal efficiency of your shop by covering its walls with wood paneling or sheet material, and filling the gap in between studs with insulation. Wood paneling in particular creates a warm, comfortable atmosphere. Interior wall covering will make your shop quieter too, since the walls will absorb some of the din of your power tools. As a bonus, you can conceal wiring behind the walls. Make sure the basement walls do not leak before covering them with insulation and paneling.

To hide the exposed joists, ducts, and wiring above your head, consider installing a ceiling. A suspended tile ceiling, in which the tiles sit in a framework of supports hanging from the joists, is one popular option. In a large shop, a dropped ceiling such as this will also help retain heat. Acoustical ceiling tiles are an inexpensive alternative; the tiles are attached to furring strips that are nailed to the joists.

SHOP TIP

Making the transition to a raised floor
If part of your shop has a raised floor, you can make a smooth transition from the lower concrete floor with several beveled 2-by-6s laid end-to-end. Cut a rabbet in one edge of each 2-by-6 to accommodate the plywood floor and the 1-by-2 grid underneath. Then bevel the opposite edge, forming a ramp to facilitate moving items from one floor to the other. Nail or screw the plywood to the 2-by-6s.

HEATING AND VENTILATION

Heating is a necessity for most shops in North America. Some woodworking tasks demand it; gluing and finishing in particular require steady temperatures. Heating your shop also makes it more comfortable and safe; numb fingers invite accidents.

If your shop is some distance from your home's furnace, a separate heating system will be needed. Many woodworkers swear by wood heat; it has the added benefit of consuming scrap pieces. Yet this means frequently feeding the stove and cleaning the chimney; insuring your shop against fire can also be a problem. Electric baseboard units are more convenient, but can contribute to high utility bills and frequently are clogged with sawdust.

Portable kerosene and propane burners should be avoided in the shop, since they use an open flame and emit toxic exhaust. Coil-type electric heaters are also a fire hazard.

Whichever heating system you choose, keep the area around it free of sawdust and place it away from the finishing and wood storage areas. And remember, any system will be improved by good ventilation.

Consider your need to control humidity. In shops in humid climates, too much moisture means an investment in a dehumidifier to keep wood dry and tools from rusting. Shops in more arid climates face the opposite dilemma and may require a humidifier.

Finally, every shop requires adequate ventilation. Airborne sawdust and toxic finishing vapors may not be as visible a danger as kickback on a table saw but the threat they pose is just as real. While fire or explosions due to high concentrations of sawdust or finishing vapors are rare, they can be devastating. A good ventilation system changes the air often enough to maintain safe levels of airborne dust and fumes. It should include dust collection equipment at each stationary power tool that produces sawdust *(page 78)*, and a general exhaust setup *(below)* to remove the dust and fumes that remain.

While window fans or bathroom-type vent models are fine for general exhaust purposes, a finishing booth or spray room requires something different: An explosion-proof tube-axial fan is recommended. Fans are rated by the amount of air that they move, measured in cubic feet per minute (cfm). Divide the cubic volume of your shop (its length times its width times its height) by 6 to find the rating needed to change the air 10 times per hour—the minimum level for safe ventilation.

VENTILATING A SHOP

Installing a general exhaust setup
If your shop does not have windows or doors to provide proper cross-ventilation, install an exhaust setup to clean the air. The system shown at left is a simple one, consisting of an air intake at one end of the shop connected to the outdoors or your home's air ducts, and an explosion-proof fan mounted in the wall at the opposite end. The intake is covered with a furnace or air-conditioning filter to clean the incoming air. The exhaust fan is placed higher than the intake, causing the air that rises to be drawn out of the shop. For best results, orient the exhaust setup along the longest axis of your shop.

WORKBENCH

The makers of this workbench capitalized on the classic lines of a centuries-old design, creating a scaled-down bench that doubles as a living room table.

The workbench is the cornerstone of the woodshop, with a history almost as old as woodworking itself. Examples of primitive workbenches have been found dating back more than 2,000 years. Woodworkers in ancient Rome advanced the basic design, devising benches with simple stops that allowed them to secure pieces of wood. Until that time, craftsmen were forced to hold their work, cutting or shaping it with one hand while chopping or planing with the other. Further improvements came slowly, however, and vises were only added centuries later.

With each refinement the workbench has assumed an increasingly indispensable role in the workshop. It is little surprise that many call the workbench the most important tool a woodworker can own.

A good workbench does not take an active role in the woodworking process—it does not cut wood or shape it—but the bench and its accoutrements perform another essential task: They free your hands and position the work so you can cut, drill, shape, and finish efficiently. In the past, even the most-used benches have fallen short of the ideal. With its massive, single-plank top, the Roubo Bench of the 18th Century was popular throughout Europe, yet it had no tail vise or bench dogs to hold a workpiece; instead, the task was done by a system of iron holdfasts and an optional leg vise. One hundred years later, the American Shakers improved on the Roubo. Their bench was a large affair that sported a laminated top, a system of bench dog holes, an L-shaped tail vise, and a leg vise. The Shaker bench was not too different from the modern cabinetmaker's bench pictured on page 46.

The design of the workbench has changed little since the early 19th Century; only its accessories and manner of assembly have been altered. In fact, some claim that the only true innovation has been inventor Ron Hickman's ubiquitous Workmate™. Developed in the 1960s, the Workmate™ revolutionized the way many people look at work surfaces, because it provided some of the clamping abilities of a standard workbench with a collapsible, portable design.

Although the Workmate™ has found a niche in workshops around the world, many woodworkers—both amateur and professional—still opt for nothing less than a solid maple or beech bench. Often they choose to build their own, believing that the care and attention paid in crafting such a bench will be reflected in their later work. The chapter that follows shows how to assemble a modern cabinetmaker's workbench, and how to install the vises and accessories needed to turn an ordinary bench into a more flexible work station.

With its origins rooted in an era without power tools, the standard cabinetmaker's bench now incorporates vises designed for use with both power and hand tools.

ANATOMY OF A WORKBENCH

The workbench shown at right is patterned after a traditional cabinetmaker's bench, and is crafted from solid maple. The bench incorporates two vises considered to be standard equipment: a face vise on the front, left-hand end of the bench, and a tail vise with a sliding dog block mounted on the opposite end.

You can build such a workbench from a kit supplied with materials and instructions. You can buy the plans for a bench and order the materials yourself. Or, you can follow the instructions presented in this chapter and construct a bench to suit your needs. Whichever route you take, a workbench is assembled in three distinct phases: the base *(page 50)*; the top *(page 53)*; and the clamping accessories—vises *(page 56)*, bench dogs, and hold-downs *(page 62)*.

The top surface of most benches is generally between 33 and 36 inches high. The height that is best for you can be determined by measuring the distance between the floor and the inside of your wrist while you stand upright with your arms at your sides.

Finish your workbench with two coats of a penetrating oil-based product, such as tung oil. Not only do these products penetrate the surface and protect the wood, but the finish can be refurbished simply by scrubbing it with steel wool and recoating.

Face vise
Also known as front vise; jaw secures work against bench

Bench dog hole
Holds a bench dog for securing work on benchtop

Arm
Supports top; top edge of arm at face-vise end relieved in same manner as feet. Usually attached to legs by mortise-and-tenon joints

Apron

Foot
Bottom edge is "relieved" with a recess for better contact with floor; ordinarily attached to the leg with mortise-and-tenon joints

Stretcher
Provides lateral stability to bench; attached to the legs in one of several ways (pages 50 and 51)

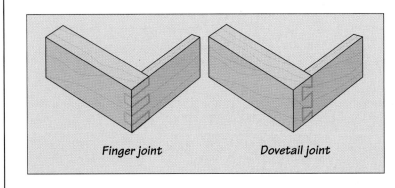

Finger joint   **Dovetail joint**

Attaching the end caps of a workbench to the aprons calls for a strong and attractive joinery method. The finger joint (also known as the box joint) and the dovetail joint shown at left are traditional favorites.

Top
Often laminated from a hard
and dense wood such as maple or
beech; boards that make up top
should be selected, prepared, and
glued up carefully to provide a
perfectly flat surface

*The workbench at left
improved the standard
design by incorporat-
ing a tilting tool chest
under the top.*

Tool tray

Bench dog
Used with tail or face vise to
clamp stock; made of metal or
wood. Tension spring keeps dog
at desired height; after use,
dog is pushed down below surface of benchtop

Sliding dog block
Connected to the tail vise screw,
this movable block contains a
bench dog that secures work
on the benchtop

End cap
Separate piece cov-
ers end grain of top
piece and supports
tail vise screw

Leg

Tail vise
Moves sliding dog block to
adjust clamping capacity
to length of work

BUILDING THE BASE

The base of a workbench typically consists of two rectangular frames connected by a pair of stretchers. The frames are essentially identical, each with a foot, an arm, and two legs. The arm of the left-hand frame is sometimes about 3 inches longer than the other arm to provide additional support for the face vise.

For a bench like the one shown on pages 48 and 49, use ⁸⁄₄ maple (1¾ inches thick after surfacing). The feet, arms and legs are made from two boards apiece face-glued together, and then reduced to the proper thickness on the jointer and planer. If you wish to build the base with mortise-and-tenons, cut four-shouldered tenons at the end of the legs and rout matching mortises in the feet and arms. Tenons are also cut at the ends of the stretchers with mortises required in the legs. The illustration

below shows a knockdown alternative to assembling the base with mortise-and-tenons.

The joints between the stretchers and the legs need to be solid, yet sufficiently flexible to be taken apart should you want to move the bench. Consequently, knockdown hardware designed for the purpose is often used to join the stretchers to the legs. The pages that follow detail some other methods of reinforcing knockdown connections.

Butt joints connecting the legs of a workbench to the stretchers can be reinforced with hardwood knockdown fittings. The fittings are inserted into mortises cut into the ends of the stretchers; matching machine bolts and nuts are then used to secure the joint.

REINFORCING KNOCKDOWN JOINERY

Using truss rods

Instead of using mortise-and-tenon joints to build the base, use butt joints reinforced by truss rods, as shown at right. Available in kits, the rods can be loosened or tightened after assembly to compensate for wood movement as a result of changes in humidity. Rout grooves for the rods into the edges of the stretchers and the inside edges of the legs; the depth and width of the channels should equal the rod's diameter. Test-assemble the base and mark the groove locations on the legs and arms. Then bore a hole at each mark, making the diameter equal to that of the rods; countersink the holes so you can drive the nuts flush with the wood surface. Assemble the base, fitting the rods into the grooves and holes, and tightening the connections with washers and nuts. Cover the grooves with solid wood inlay if you wish to conceal the rods.

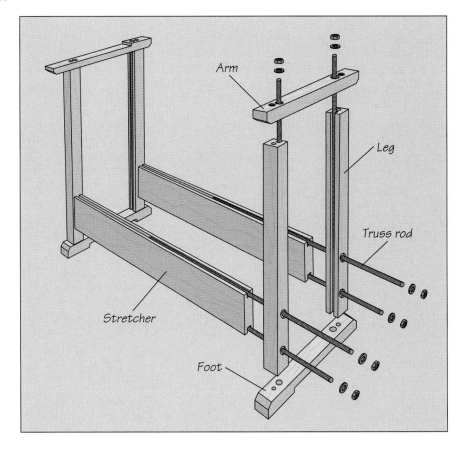

Arm

Leg

Truss rod

Stretcher

Foot

Using machine bolts and wood blocks

To reinforce the connection between the legs and stretchers, glue a wood block of the same thickness as the stock to each edge of the stretchers. The blocks will increase the contact area between the stretchers and the legs. Once the glue is dry, cut a tenon at the end of each stretcher and a matching mortise in the leg. Fit the pieces together and bore two holes for machine bolts through the leg and the tenon in the blocks; countersink the holes. Make the connection fast by fitting the bolts into the holes, slipping on washers and tightening the nuts *(right)*.

Stretcher

Leg

Block

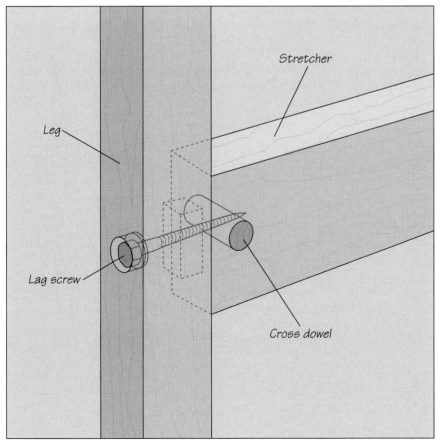

Stretcher

Leg

Lag screw

Cross dowel

Using lag screws and dowels

Another way to strengthen a mortise-and-tenon joint between the stretchers and legs is shown at left. Cut a 1-inch-diameter hardwood dowel to a length equal to the thickness of the stretcher. Then bore a 1-inch-diameter hole through the stretcher about $1\frac{1}{2}$ inches from its end. Also bore a hole for a lag screw through the leg, stopping the drill when the bit reaches the hole in the stretcher; countersink the hole so the screw head will sit flush with the surface. Fit the stretcher tenon into the leg mortise, tap the dowel into place in the stretcher, and drive the screw. Choose a screw that is long enough to bite through the dowel.

PREPARING THE FEET

Outfeed table

Infeed table

Stop block

Clamp

Relieving the feet
Once you are satisfied with the fit of the parts of the base, disassemble the stretchers and legs and relieve the feet on the jointer. Install a clamp on the jointer's infeed table to hold the guard out of the way during the operation. Set both the infeed and outfeed tables for a 1/16-inch depth of cut, and clamp stop blocks to both tables to guide the beginning and end of the cut. To make the first pass, lower the foot onto the knives, keeping it flush against the fence and the stop block on the infeed table. Feed the foot across the knives *(left)* until it contacts the stop block on the outfeed table. Keep both hands well above the cutterhead. Make as many passes as necessary to complete the recess, lowering the tables 1/16 inch at a time, and readjusting the stop blocks as necessary.

T-nut

Leveler

Installing adjustable levelers
To level a workbench on an uneven shop floor, install adjustable levelers in the feet. Each leveler consists of a T-nut and a threaded portion with a plastic tip *(inset)*. Bore two holes into the bottom of the foot near each end. Make the hole's diameter equal to that of the T-nut and its length slightly longer than the threaded section. Tap the T-nuts into the holes and screw in the levelers *(right)*. Once the bench is assembled, adjust the levelers until the benchtop is level.

BUILDING THE TOP

One of the most important features of a workbench is a perfectly flat top. At one time, a benchtop could be built of solid maple or beech boards 12 inches wide and 2 inches thick. But today such planks are difficult to come by, and benchtop slabs are built up from narrow boards, layers of plywood sandwiched between strips of hardwood, or laminated plywood strips sheathed in hardboard. However, edge gluing solid wood boards together butcher-block style, as shown below, is the time-honored method.

Cut from ⁸/₄ stock, the boards are glued together first, then the slab is cut to length. To minimize warping, arrange the pieces so that the end grain is reversed. Also make sure the face grain of all the boards runs in the same direction. This will make it easier to plane the top surface of the slab smooth.

After gluing up the slab, prepare the dog blocks. They are glued up from a length of ⁸/₄ stock and one of ⁴/₄ stock with the bench holes dadoed out of the thicker board. The sliding dog block for the tail vise is sawn off before the front rail and fixed block are glued together *(page 54)*. Next, the slab, fixed dog block, and rear rail are glued up *(page 55)*; hardwood keys and plywood splines are used to strengthen the connections.

After the sliding dog block, tool tray, and aprons are installed, the final step involves attaching the end caps to the top. Two connections are used: The caps are bolted to the slab and joined to the aprons by means of dovetail or finger joints.

Once the top of a bench is installed on the base, a straightedge held on edge across the surface can be used to check it for flatness.

ANATOMY OF A BENCHTOP

Tool tray bottom

Spline

Back apron

Sliding dog block

Top slab

Back rail

Recess for machine bolt

Front apron

End cap

Front rail

Hardwood keys

Fixed dog block

PREPARING THE FIXED DOG BLOCK

Bench dog hole

Bench dog

Cutting the bench dog holes

Bench dogs are fabricated from two boards, so it is simple to cut the dog holes in the thicker piece before glue-up. Two steps are involved. First, cut a row of evenly spaced dadoes wide enough to accept the dogs; angle the fixed-block dadoes slightly toward the tail vise, and the sliding-block dadoes away from the tail vise so that the dogs will grip the work firmly when clamping pressure is applied. Next, clamp the board to a work surface and use a chisel to notch the top of each dado to accept the dog heads *(left)*. That way, the dogs can be pushed down flush with the bench surface when they are not in use. Now the two parts can be glued up to form the finished blocks.

BUILD IT YOURSELF

A JIG FOR DRILLING BENCH DOG HOLES
If you plan to use round bench dogs, you can use the shop-made jig shown below to bore their holes after you glue up the bench top. The jig should be about 10 inches long; the lip is cut from a 1-by-2 and the base from a 1-by-4. After screwing them together, bore guide holes about 8 inches apart and 3 inches from the lip. The holes should accommodate the dogs you will use.

To use the jig, clamp it to the right end of the dog block so the lip is against the front edge and the right-hand guide hole is over the position of the first dog hole. Using the guide holes, bore the first two holes in the bench. For each subsequent hole, remove the clamp and slide the jig to the left until the right-hand guide hole is aligned with the last hole bored. Slip a bench dog through the holes, clamp the jig and bore the left-hand hole *(right)*. Repeat the process until you are finished boring all the holes.

Round bench dog

Base

Lip

ASSEMBLING THE BENCHTOP

1 Gluing up the top

First, glue up the top slab. Before gluing up the benchtop, rout grooves on both sides of the dog blocks and front rail, on one face of the front apron and back rail, and along the edges and ends of the top slab. Cut matching keys and splines. Refer to the drawing on page 53 for the size and placement of the grooves, keys, and splines. If you want to incorporate a tool tray in your bench, cut ½-inch rabbets into the bottom edges of the back rail and apron; later in the assembly process you will fit a piece of ½-inch plywood to form the tray. Set aside the sliding dog block (with the hardwood keys glued in place) and front and back aprons, spread glue on all mating surfaces, and clamp *(right)*, alternating the bar or pipe clamps on the top and bottom of the work.

2 Attaching the end caps

The end caps can be applied while the tail vise is being installed *(page 57)*. When that is done, invert the benchtop and rout a T-shaped recess at each end, centered between the edges. Cut two rectangular fittings from scrap hardwood so that they fit in the base of each recess. Notch one side of each fitting to accept a ⅜-inch nut, and place a fitting and nut in each recess. Set the end caps in position and mark where they contact the recesses. At each mark bore a hole for a ⅜-inch bolt, counterboring so the bolt heads are flush. Rout a groove in each end cap to accept the plywood spline, and rout a ½-inch rabbet on the bottom inside edge of the back rail to accept the tool tray. Install the tail vise on the right-hand end cap *(page 57)*. Spread glue on the contacting surfaces, fit the end caps *(left)*, and bolt them in place *(inset)*. Finally, fit the front and rear aprons and tool tray and clamp.

VISES AND ACCESSORIES

Vises are the tools that transform the workbench from a simple, flat surface into a versatile work station. The modern woodworking bench incorporates two types of vise: the face vise that secures work to the front edge of the bench, and the tail vise that uses wood or metal bench dogs to secure work on the top of the bench. The pages that follow examine ways of installing both the tail vise *(page 57)* and face vise *(page 58)*.

Face vises made entirely of wood are rare. However, a wooden vise is preferable to a metal type because wooden jaws can grip work without marring its surface. A good compromise can be reached by buying the hardware for a metal vise and mounting wooden face blocks. You can extend the capacity of a face vise by boring holes in the benchtop and securing work between a bench dog in the vise's jaws and one inserted in one of the holes.

Tail vises are available in two types: an enclosed model that incorporates a sliding dog block *(below and page 57)* and one that features an L-shaped block, as in the photo at left. Some tail vises extend across the entire end of a workbench and have two screws; these are known as end vises, and they extend the utility of an already versatile tool.

Some tail vises, like the one shown at left, incorporate an L-shaped shoulder block. The block allows work to be clamped between the rear jaw of the vise and the end of the bench.

ANATOMY OF A TAIL VISE

Fixed dog block

Apron

End cap

Sliding dog block

Vise flange

Vise collar

Vise screw

INSTALLING A TAIL VISE

1 Installing the vise hardware

To install a tail vise on a bench with a sliding dog block, position the vise collar against the right-hand side end cap and outline the hole for the vise screw. Then set a support board on the drill press table and clamp the end cap on top of it. Fit the drill press with a spade bit slightly larger than the vise screw and bore a hole through the end cap *(near right)*. Screw the vise collar to the end cap so the two holes line up. Next, secure the sliding dog block end-up in handscrews and clamp the handscrews to a work surface. Position the vise flange on the block and mark its screw holes. Bore a pilot hole at each mark, then screw the flange to the block *(far right)*.

End cap

Support board

Vise flange

Sliding dog block

Rail

Hardwood key

Apron

2 Assembling the vise

Fit the sliding dog block in the bench so the hardwood keys in the block run in the grooves in the sides of the rail. Thread the vise screw through the vise collar, test-fit the end cap on the benchtop and lock the ball joint on the end of the screw into the vise flange. Set the front apron in position against the dog blocks *(left)* and test the movement of the vise by turning the screw. If the sliding block binds, remove the end cap, apron, and sliding dog block, and ease the fit by paring the keys with a chisel. Once you are satisfied with the vise's movement, attach the aprons, end caps, and trays following the procedures outlined on page 55.

ANATOMY OF A FACE VISE

Fixed
dog block

Vise carriage

Guide
rod

Apron

Guide rod
bushing

Face block

Arm

Vise screw

Support
block

Faceplate

INSTALLING A FACE VISE

1 **Preparing the face block**
Cut an 18-inch-long ¾-by-3½ inch
hardwood support block and screw it in
place under the front left corner of the
bench, after boring a row of clearance
holes for the bench dogs. Next, build
up the face block by gluing two pieces of
⁸⁄₄ hardwood together; cut it to a final size
of 5-by-18 inches. To mark and bore the
holes for the vise screw and guide rods,
mark a line across the face of the face
block; offset the line from the top edge by
the thickness of the benchtop slab (not the
front apron depth). Now use the carriage
as a template: Center its top edge on
the line and use a brad-point bit to accu-
rately mark the position of the three
holes *(right)* and bore them.

Vise carriage

Brad-
point bit

Face
block

2 Preparing the bench

Once the holes have been drilled through the face block, transfer their location to the workbench apron. Set the face block and benchtop on sawhorses and use bar clamps to hold the block in position against the apron; protect the stock with wood pads. Make sure the top edge of the block is flush with the bench-top and its end is flush with the end cap. Mark the hole locations on the apron using the brad-point bit *(right)*. Remove the face block and bore the holes through the apron and bench dog block.

3 Mounting the vise

Attach the vise assembly—the face-plate, screw, and guide rods—to the face block. Turn the benchtop upside down, place the vise carriage on the bench's underside, and feed the vise screw and guide rods through the holes in the apron and into the carriage. Make pilot holes on the underside of the bench and fasten the carriage in place. Next, fasten the guide rod bushings to the apron: Remove the vise assembly, fit the bushings on the rods, remount the assembly, and outline the bushings' location on the apron. Then remove the vise assembly again and secure the benchtop so the apron is fac-ing up. With a router and straight bit, cut recesses for the bushings within the out-lines *(left)*. Screw the bushings to the recesses in the apron and attach the vise to the bench. Now the workbench top is ready to be attached to the base. Lay the top upside down on the floor, place the base in position, and drive lag screws through the arms into the top.

JIGS FOR IRON-JAWED BENCH VISES

Basic auxiliary jaw

Tapered vise jaw

V-groove vise jaw

Fitting wooden inserts to metal jaws

If your bench is equipped with a metal-jawed vise like the one shown at the top of page 61, fitting interchangeable auxiliary jaws can extend the vise's versatility. The wooden inserts shown above will not only be less damaging to workpieces than metal jaws, but they can also be custom-made for special jobs. Each insert is made from ½-inch-thick solid stock with a rabbeted 1-by-1 block glued at each end to hug the ends of the vise jaw. Although a pair is required, only one of each sample is illustrated. The basic jaw *(above, left)* will do most standard clamping jobs. The tapered jaw *(above, center)* features a wedge-shaped strip for holding tapered stock efficiently. The V-groove jaw *(above, right)* includes a strip with a groove cut down its middle for securing cylindrical work.

SHOP TIP

A quick-switch vise
If you are reluctant to bolt your bench vise onto your workbench, attach it instead to a T-shaped base made of ¾-inch plywood. Join the two pieces of the base together with a dado joint and screws. Secure the vertical part of the base in either the tail or face vise of the bench.

A SLIDING BENCH STOP

If your "workbench" is a standard table with a bench vise fastened to one edge, the jig and fence shown at right can lend it some versatility. Cut the auxiliary vise jaws from 1-inch stock and the pieces of the T-shaped vise jig from ¾-inch wood. You will need two pieces for the jig: a top and a lip. Rout a dado across one auxiliary jaw to accommodate the lip of the vise jig and another on the underside of the jig top. Screw the auxiliary jaws to the vise jaws, making a cut for the vise screw if necessary, then glue and screw the lip to the top of the jig. Cut the sliding fence from ½-inch-thick stock and cut two stopped grooves through it for ¼-inch carriage bolts. To mount the fence, bore two holes through the table for the bolts, feed the bolts through the holes and the grooves and fasten them with

Top

Sliding fence

Lip

Auxiliary
vise jaw

washers and wing nuts. To use the jig and fence, slide the lip into the auxiliary jaw, adjust the sliding fence to hold the workpiece snugly and clamp it in place by tightening the vise jaw and wing nuts.

PREVENTING VISE RACKING

Using a stepped block

When securing a workpiece at one end of a face vise, the other end of the vise is likely to rack—or tilt toward the bench—and cause the work to slip. To prevent racking, use a stepped hardwood block to keep the jaws square. Cut a series of steps in one face of the block, spacing them at equal intervals, such as ½ inch. Place the block in the open end of the vise at the same time you are securing the workpiece so that the vise is parallel to the edge of the bench *(left)*.

BENCH DOGS AND HOLD DOWNS

Bench dogs are as important as vises in maximizing the flexibility and utility of a well-designed workbench. A set of bench dogs works like a second pair of hands to secure workpieces for planing, chiseling, mortising, carving, or other woodworking tasks.

Although the bench dog looks like a deceptively simple peg, it incorporates design features that enable it to hold a workpiece firmly without slipping in its hole. One feature usually is a thin metal spring attached to one side that presses against the inside wall of the dog hole in the workbench. To help strengthen the grip of bench dogs, the holes are also angled toward the vise at 4°.

Bench dogs can be either round or square. Round dogs are easier to incorporate in a bench that does not yet have dog holes; it is simpler to bore holes than to make square dog holes. Since round dogs can swivel, their notched, flat heads enable them to clamp stock in practically any direction. This can be a disadvantage: Some woodworkers claim that round dogs tend to slip in their holes more than square dogs, which cannot rotate.

Bench dogs can be made of either metal or wood. Metal dogs have a weight, strength, and stiffness that wooden ones cannot match. Yet wooden dogs have their advantages—as any woodworker who has nicked a plane blade on a metal dog will attest.

Bench dogs are not the only method of securing stock; bench hooks, carving hooks, wedges, and hold downs are also useful for keeping stock in place. The following pages illustrate a number of commercial and shop-made options to keep workpieces put while you work.

This bench dog features a threaded screw that converts it into a miniature tail vise. Used in conjunction with other bench dogs, it excels at clamping small or irregular work, like the panel shown above.

BENCH DOGS

Tongue

Kerf

Making a wooden bench dog

Bench dogs can be crafted from hardwood stock; the one shown at left uses an angled wooden tongue as a spring. Cut the dog to fit the holes in your workbench, then chisel out a dado from the middle of the dog. Saw a short kerf into the lower corner of the dado, angling the cut so the tongue will extend beyond the edge of the dado. Cut the tongue from hardwood, making it about as long as the dado, as wide as the dog, and as thick as the kerf. Glue the tongue in the kerf.

Making a spring-loaded bench dog

A wooden bench dog can be made to fit snugly by equipping it with a metal spring cut from an old band saw or hacksaw blade. Cut your dog to size, then chisel out a small recess for the spring. The width and depth of the recess should equal the width and thickness of the spring, but its length should be slightly shorter than that of the spring. Press the spring into the recess; the metal will bow outward, holding the dog firmly in its hole.

BUILD IT YOURSELF

SHOP-MADE EDGE DOGS

Edge dogs like those shown at right are ideal for securing a workpiece along the edge of your bench. They feature a round dowel at one end that drops into a bench dog hole and angled heads that butt up against the edge of the bench and hold the work.

Start by cutting the dogs from hardwood stock. Both left-hand and right-hand dogs are needed, with the heads angled in opposing directions. Bore a $\frac{1}{2}$-inch-diameter hole through the ends, and drive a 3-inch length of dowel in each hole. Then insert the dowel in a bench dog hole and angle the dog so it extends beyond the edge of the table. Mark a 90° notch for the head perpendicular to the edge of the bench and cut it out. To hold the edge dog in place when clamping pressure is applied, saw a $\frac{1}{4}$-inch-slice off the

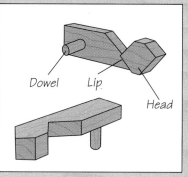

bottom of the dog, except for the head. This provides a lip that will butt against the edge of the bench (left).

To use the edge dogs, place the left-hand dog in a hole in the fixed dog block and the right-hand one in the sliding dog block of the tail vise. Tighten the vise until the workpiece is held in the notches (below).

Edge dog
$\frac{3}{4}" \times 2\frac{1}{4}" \times 8"$

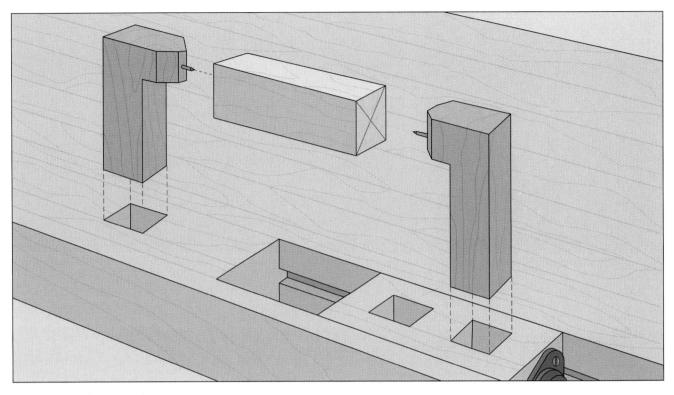

Making and setting up carving dogs

Using a standard bench dog as a model, you can fashion a pair of customized dogs that will grip a carved or turned workpiece, or secure irregular-sized work, such as mitered molding. To make these accessories, cut bevels on either side of the head of a standard bench dog and drive a small screw or nail into the center of the head; snip off the fastener's head to form a sharp point. To use the devices, place one dog in a dog hole of the bench's fixed dog block and the other in the tail vise or a sliding dog block hole *(above)*. Tighten the vise screw until the points contact the ends of the workpiece and hold it securely.

SHOP TIP

Carving screws
A pair of hanger bolts can enable you to secure an irregular-shaped workpiece, such as a carving block, to your bench. The bolts feature wood screw threads on one end and machine screw threads on the other. To secure a workpiece, bore two holes through the benchtop for the bolts. Screw the bolts into the carving block from underneath the top and hold the bolts to the underside of the top with washers and wing nuts.

HOLD-DOWNS AND BENCH STOPS

Holding bolt

Notch

Using a hold-down clamp

Commercial hold-down clamps can be used alone or with bench dogs to secure a workpiece in place anywhere on a workbench. The type shown features an adjustable holding bolt which sits in a counterbored hole through the benchtop *(inset)*. To use the clamp, raise the bolt head and slide it through the notch at the base of the clamp. Set the workpiece under the clamp jaw and tighten the screw *(above)*. (In the illustration, a wood pad is being used to apply equal pressure to both stiles of a door frame.) To remove the clamp from the bench, slide it off the bolt head and let the bolt drop below the surface of the top.

Wood pad

Hold-down clamp

Wedge

Bench stop

Making and using a temporary bench stop

A clamped-on bench stop cut from ¾-inch plywood will secure a workpiece to the benchtop without the help of bench dogs. Cut the bench stop to size, then mark out a triangular wedge, typically 3 inches shorter than the stop. Cut out the wedge and set it aside. To use the bench stop, clamp it to the benchtop and slide the workpiece into the notch, butting one side against the straight edge of the notch. Secure the piece with the wedge, tapping it tightly in place with a mallet *(left)*.

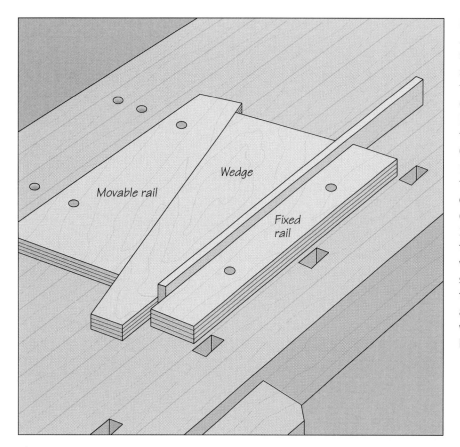

Installing a wedge stop

A wedge stop can also be used to secure stock on a benchtop *(left)*. The stop consists of a fixed rail and a movable rail that are secured by dowels resting in a double row of holes bored into the workbench. Together with a triangular wedge, the rails keep a workpiece from moving. Cut the rails and the wedge from ¾-inch plywood. (You can choose thicker stock for the rails, depending on the thickness of your workpiece.) Bore two ½-inch-diameter holes in each rail, then glue a 2-inch-long dowel in each hole. Bore two rows of ½-inch-diameter holes in the workbench for the dowels. To use the stop, place the fixed rail at one end of the row of holes and the movable rail the appropriate distance away so the wedge, when positioned between the rails, will keep the workpiece steady.

Making a bench hook

The shop-built jig shown at right will ensure that the crosscuts you make on the workbench will be square. Use ¾-inch plywood for the base and strips of 2-by-2 stock for the lips. Make the base at least as long as the width of your workpiece and wide enough to support it. Screw the lips to the guide, attaching one to each face. To use the jig, butt one lip against the edge of the bench and press the workpiece firmly against the other. Align the cutting line with the edge of the base and make the cut *(inset)*.

Making a flip-up stop

The flip-up bench stop shown at right pro-vides another way to make quick guided crosscuts on a workbench. Cut the two pieces of the stop from hardwood. Screw the pieces to the end of the benchtop; on the bench shown, the inner edge of the pivoting piece is lined up with the edge of the tool tray to provide a convenient reference line for squaring up a crosscut. Screw the stationary piece in place with two screws, and the flip-up piece with one so that it can pivot. When not in use, the pivoting piece should lie on edge atop the stationary piece. To use the stop, flip up the pivoting piece, butt the workpiece against it, and make your crosscut.

Flip-up piece

Stationary piece

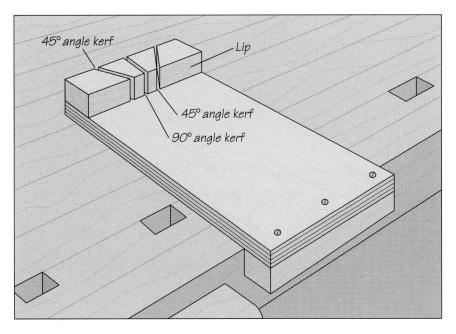

45° angle kerf

Lip

45° angle kerf

90° angle kerf

Making and using a miter bench hook

Customize a standard bench hook to make 45° angle miter cuts by adding kerfs to one of the lips. Build a bench hook *(page 66)*, then use a backsaw to cut two kerfs in the lip at opposing 45° angles and one at 90° *(left)*. Use the miter bench hook as you would a standard bench hook, lining up the cutting line on the workpiece with the desired kerf.

SHOP ACCESSORIES

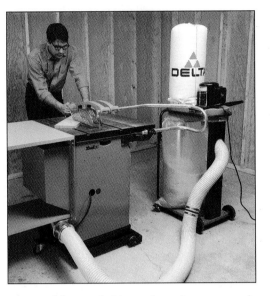

Most of the wood chips and sawdust generated by this 10-inch table saw are captured by a portable dust collection system. Often neglected in the past, dust collection has become a central concern of many safety-conscious woodworkers in planning the layout of their shops.

Look beneath the surface of an efficient, well-equipped shop, and you will find several invisible auxiliaries: accessories designed to make the work safer and the shop more comfortable in which to work. The most commonly found helpers are compressors, generators, bench grinders, and—perhaps the most important for safety and comfort—dust collection systems.

Air compressors first were utilized by woodworkers only for finishing work—to apply lacquer and varnish more smoothly than with a brush. But with the advent of such tools as pneumatic nailers, compressors are found more frequently, even in small home workshops. Air-powered tools are discussed starting on page 72.

Generators, too, are finding a place, especially among those woodworkers who take their craft away from home and power lines. They are explored on page 74.

Grinders, of course, can speed tool sharpening. More importantly, as you will see on page 76, they can permit you to modify tools and reclaim damaged cutting edges.

Airborne dust once was considered an unavoidable consequence of working with wood. But the increased emphasis on environmental health has led to the introduction of efficient dust collection systems that are affordable to home woodworkers. They should be a high priority item for every home workshop. Tiny wood dust particles can remain in the shop for more than an hour after the tool has been used. The dust poses several health risks. If the wood contains toxins or irritants—and many species do *(see back endpapers)*—the effects can lead to a wide range of ailments, including dermatitis, shortness of breath, and dizziness. Recent studies have shown that long-term inhalation of wood dust is at least a contributing factor in cancers of the tongue, tonsils, lung, and larynx.

When you add to the equation the fire risk and the hazard of a dust-covered shop floor, there are compelling reasons for installing some kind of dust collection system in your shop. Pages 78 to 87 provide you with information you will need to set up and maintain both central and portable systems. Remember that designing a central system requires careful attention to detail and precise calculation of your specific requirements. To be safe, check your plans and figures with an engineer before installing the system.

Hooked up to a compressor, this air-powered sander is compact enough to hold in one hand, yet it smooths wood as efficiently as an electric sander.

Planers can create a substantial mound of sawdust in short order. A portable dust collector will keep most of the dust from this and other power tools off the shop floor and out of the air.

High-volume, low-pressure (HVLP) spray system
For applying stains and finishes. Features electric turbine that supplies large amount of air at low pressure through air hose to spray gun; compared to conventional, compressed-air type systems, HVLP allows higher percentage of finish to contact workpiece

Multitester
Also known as volt-ohmmeter, or VOM. Battery-powered tool used in troubleshooting and repairing electric devices; measures resistance and AC or DC voltage in a circuit

Air compressor
Supplies stream of high pressure air through hose to power a variety of air-operated tools, such as sanders, spray guns, and drills; consumer-grade models range from $\frac{1}{8}$ to 5 horsepower and can generate up to 200 pounds per square inch (psi) of air pressure and 0.3 to 15 cubic feet of air per minute (cfm).

Generator

Typically gasoline-powered, featuring up to four 120- and 240-volt outlets. Motors on consumer-grade generators range between 3 and 8 horsepower and produce 500 to 4000 watts of output; most models weigh less than 130 pounds and can be fitted with wheels for easy portability

Shop vacuum

Cleans up dust and liquid spills; hose can be attached to individual tools to collect dust as it is produced. Typically features 1 ¼- to 2 ½-inch-diameter collection hose and 5- to 10-gallon tank; some models can double as portable blower

Bench grinder

Coarse wheel (left) squares, sharpens, and smooths blades and bits; cloth wheel (right) polishes and cleans. Features a ¼- to ½-horsepower electric motor; eye shields, adjustable tool rests, and wheel guards standard on most models. Benchtop grinders usually bolted to work surface

Wheel dresser

Used to true or reshape bench grinder wheel. Star-wheel dresser (above) uses up to four star-shaped wheels; diamond-point dresser (below) features ¼-carat diamond set in bronze tip and metal shaft

AIR COMPRESSORS

An air compressor can be fitted with a large number of tools and attachments, making it a convenient shop accessory. In some shops, a compressor can represent an alternative to some electric tools. For others, it can be a valuable supplement.

Pneumatic drills, grinders, sanders, and wrenches perform at least as effectively as their electric-powered counterparts. Some tools, like sprayers, nailers, and abrasive cleaners, are clearly superior to the alternatives.

Compressors and the tools they drive are inherently simple: The air is drawn in, pressurized by a diaphragm or one or more pistons, and usually stored in a tank. When the trigger on an air-driven tool is pressed, the air travels through a hose to power the tool.

Because they contain no heavy electric motor, most air tools are lighter, cheaper, and easier to repair than their cousins. They cannot overheat, and there is no danger of electrical shock.

Compressed-air power does have some drawbacks, chiefly the cost of the compressor itself and maintenance. Air drills and the like must be oiled daily. And you will invest several hundred dollars in a compressor that is capable of driving typical shop tools.

Some air-powered tools require a sizable volume of air, usually measured in cubic feet per minute (cfm); others need a minimum level of air pressure in pounds per square inch (psi). When choosing a compressor, consider the cfm or psi requirements of the air-powered tools you plan to use and buy a compressor with slightly more power. You never know when you will want to expand your tool inventory.

Air-powered tools work best at a specific pressure indicated in the owner's manual for the particular tool. Before starting a job, the compressor's air regulator should be adjusted to the proper setting for the task at hand.

AIR-POWERED TOOLS AND ACCESSORIES

Jitterbug sander
Orbital sander capable of producing 2500 strokes per minute; weighs less than 5 pounds. Requires 6.5 cfm at 90 psi; must be used with tank-mounted compressor with at least 3 horsepower

Drill
⅜-inch drill that turns bits at 2500 rpm; weighs only 2¼ pounds. Requires 3 cfm at 90 psi; must be used with tank-mounted compressor with at least ¾ horsepower

Spray gun
Heavy-duty sprayer with adjustable fluid and air controls. Requires 5.5 cfm at 40 psi; can be used with any compressor with more than 1 horsepower

COMPRESSOR SAFETY TIPS

• Read your owner's manual carefully before operating a compressor or any air-powered tool.

• Do not reset any switches or valves on the compressor; they have been preset at safe levels at the factory.

• Check the hoses, plugs, wires, pipes, and tubes of the compressor, and the tool air inlets before each use. Do not use the compressor or tool if any part is worn or damaged.

• Wear safety glasses and hearing protection when using air-powered tools.

• Do not exceed the pressure rating of an air tool or accessory.

• Always plug a compressor into a grounded outlet of the appropriate amperage.

• Relieve pressure slowly when depressurizing the tank.

• Do not press the trigger of an air tool when connecting it to an air hose.

• Do not remove the belt guard of a belt-driven compressor when the machine is operating.

• Turn the compressor off if it produces an unfamiliar noise or vibration, produces insufficient air pressure, or consumes excessive oil; have the machine serviced before resuming operations.

• Allow the compressor to cool before performing any maintenance; wear gloves to disconnect any parts that are still hot.

• Turn the compressor off before moving it.

• Do not touch the compressor while using it or immediately after; the machine can become very hot.

• Drain any moisture from the tank after each use to prevent rust; tank pressure should be no higher than 10 psi when draining it.

• Replace the tank if it has any pin holes, rust spots, or weak spots at welds.

Brad finishing nailer
Nail gun for driving ⅜- to 1¼-inch No. 18 finishing nails; weighs less than 3 pounds. Narrow nose sets nails without marring workpiece; magazine holds up to 110 nails. Requires .28 cfm at 90 psi to drive 10 nails per minute; must be used with compressor with at least ½ horsepower

Router
¼-inch direct-drive router that turns bits at 20,000 rpm; weighs just over 1 pound. Features neoprene rubber grip to reduce vibration. Requires 90 psi; will function with most compressors

Hose connector
Joins air tool to compressor or connects two lengths of compressor hose together

Quick coupler
Used with hose connectors to attach air tools to compressor hose or to join lengths of compressor hose together; automatically shuts off air when uncoupled from compressor

PORTABLE GENERATORS

The average home and shop is so well equipped with electric fixtures, outlets, and extension cords that it is easy to take for granted the essential role that electricity plays in our lives. Yet a power outage can quickly remind you of that role. At such a time, a portable AC generator becomes an indispensable accessory for your home, your shop, or in a remote cabin where power lines do not reach.

AC, or alternating current, generators typically feature a gasoline motor that drives an alternator. Models are available with motors ranging from 3 to 8 horsepower, producing 500 to 4000 watts of power.

There are several factors to consider when selecting a generator, and the chart on page 75 can help guide you. The generator must produce enough power to start and run the tools and any other electrical devices you plug into it. The wattage ratings listed on the chart are typical. You should refer to the actual rating of your tool, which is usually printed on the tool body. If not, you can calculate the rating by multiplying the tool's amperage rating by the voltage. (For example, a 3-amp tool operating on 120 volts would have a wattage rating of 360.)

The wattage rating of a generator refers to its continuous running wattage.

Although all models feature a surge or maximum rating as much as 25 percent higher than the running value, you should rely on the running wattage rating when choosing a generator. A generator with more power than you need will run more smoothly for longer stretches and require less maintenance.

Most generators are equipped with one to four 120-volt outlets. Many models also have a 240-volt outlet and a 12-volt DC output for charging batteries.

Make sure that any generator you buy is equipped with an effective muffler. Also check the size of the fuel tank. The generator should be able to run for at least 90 minutes on a full tank.

Portable generators are a handy source of electricity during power outages or in locations where a conventional electrical supply is unavailable. Rated at 3500 watts, this model is able to drive virtually any electric workshop tool or appliance.

TYPICAL POWER TOOL WATTAGE RATINGS

Tool	Watts (Start-up)	Watts (Running)
Air compressor (¾-hp)	4000	2000
Table saw (10")	4000	1500
Saber saw	2500	1200
Circular saw (7¼")	2500	1200
Circular saw (6½")	2200	1000
Belt sander	1500	600
Bench grinder (½-hp)	1500	1200
Orbital sander	900	360
Router	900	700
Electric drill (½")	800	600
Electric drill (⅜")	600	350
Power plane	600	450
Electric drill (¼")	500	250
Random-orbit sander	500	360
HVLP spray system	400	240

Choosing a generator with a suitable wattage rating

All electric tools require more power to start up than for continuous running. The chart at left gives typical power requirements for a number of tools. When selecting a generator, make sure its wattage rating is higher than the start-up wattage of your most powerful tool. Add a safety margin of about 20 percent to the combined running wattage of all tools you will plug into the device and operate at the same time.

GENERATOR SAFETY TIPS

• Read your owner's manual carefully before operating a generator.

• Never run a generator indoors; like any internal combustion engine, it produces carbon monoxide fumes that are deadly in a confined space.

• Do not fill the generator's fuel tank while the motor is running or hot.

• Add fuel to the fuel tank at least 10 feet from your work area and any sources of heat or flames. Do not fill the tank right to the brim; the fuel can expand and overflow.

• Do not smoke while filling the fuel tank.

• Clean up any gas or oil spills immediately, wiping up the area with a clean cloth, or soaking it up with an absorbent material such as cat litter or vermiculite; avoid using sawdust, which is combustible. Place fuel-soaked rags in sealed metal containers and dispose of them following local environmental regulations.

• Do not remove any safety guards, covers, or screens from the generator while the machine is operating.

• Keep gas and oil only in containers designed specifically for fuel storage and clearly marked FUEL. Keep the containers away from sources of heat and flames.

• Check the engine oil level each time you refuel the generator.

• Check the generator's fuel lines and connections regularly; if you notice any leakage, turn the machine off and have it serviced before resuming operations.

• Never use a generator with a faulty or damaged exhaust system.

• Ground the generator following the manufacturer's instructions; this will divert any stray current from a short circuit to ground, reducing the risk of electrical shock.

• Do not connect a 240-volt tool or appliance to a 120-volt receptacle.

• Do not overload the generator by plugging in power tools or appliances with higher wattage ratings than that of the generator.

• Never wire the generator to the electrical system of your home or shop in an attempt to provide power during an outage. This practice, known as "backfeeding," is unlawful in some areas, as it poses a risk to anyone working on the electrical system.

• Keep your hands and face away from carburetor whenever the air cleaner has been removed; a sudden backfire—or explosion of fuel in an engine cylinder—can cause serious burns.

• Do not touch the generator engine or exhaust piping while the machine is running or immediately after turning it off; these parts can become very hot. Allow the generator to cool before performing any maintenance.

• Turn the generator off before performing any maintenance on it; also disconnect the spark plug wire and the battery to prevent accidental startup of the motor.

• Generator use is regulated by federal and state legislation in some areas; contact the appropriate authorities in your community for any applicable laws.

BENCH GRINDERS

From dressing and shaping metal to squaring and sharpening bits, plane irons, and chisel blades, the bench grinder is an invaluable workshop maintenance tool. Grinders are classified according to their wheel diameter. The 5- to 7-inch benchtop models, with ¼- to ½-horsepower motors, are the most popular home workshop sizes. They can be mounted on a work surface or fastened to a separate stand.

Grinding wheels come in many grits and compositions. Medium 36- and 60-grit aluminum oxide wheels will handle most tasks adequately, but you may need a finer wheel, with either 100 or 120 grit, for delicate sharpening jobs. Buffing wheels for polishing metal, and wire wheels for removing rust and cleaning metal, are also worth owning.

Most grinders operate at one speed, or allow a choice of two speeds—typically 2950 and 3600 rpm. Some newer models offer variable speeds, a particularly valuable option for polishing and

A grinder is the best tool for restoring the correct bevel angle on a nicked or out-of-square chisel blade. The tip of the blade must contact the grinder wheel at an angle of 25° to 30°.

cleaning, and for grinding with speeds low enough to maintain the temper of a steel tool.

No grinder should be used without lowering the guard mounted above each wheel; the tool should also come equipped with adjustable tool rests and wheel covers sheathing 75 percent to 80 percent of the wheels. More expensive grinders may have other features, such as spark arresters, a water tray for cooling tool tips, and exhaust outlets.

Check your grinder wheels regularly for fractures and, as the wheel wears, adjust the distance between the tool rest and the grinding wheel to about ¼ inch. A grinding wheel will eventually become dull and clogged with metal particles, and its edges may go out-of-square. As shown below, a wheel dresser is a special tool that is used to true the working face of a grinding wheel and square its edges.

DRESSING A GRINDER WHEEL

Truing the wheel
To true a grinder wheel and square its edges, use a star-wheel dresser or a diamond-point dresser. For the star-wheel dresser, move the grinder's tool rest away from the wheel. With the guard in position, switch on the grinder and butt the tip of the dresser against the wheel. Then, with your index finger resting against the tool rest, move the dresser side-to-side across the wheel *(right)*. For the diamond-point dresser, hold the device between the index finger and thumb of one hand, set it on the tool rest, and advance it toward the wheel until your index finger contacts the tool rest *(inset)*. Slide the tip of the dresser across the wheel, pressing lightly while keeping your finger on the tool rest. For either dresser, continue until the edges of the wheel are square and you have exposed fresh abrasive.

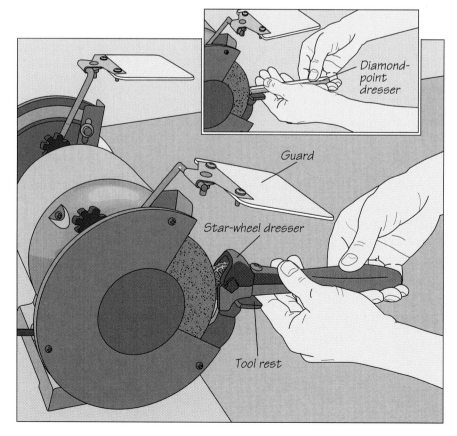

Diamond-point dresser

Guard

Star-wheel dresser

Tool rest

GOUGE-SHARPENING JIG

The jig shown at right guarantees that the tip of a gouge will contact the wheel of your grinder at the correct angle to restore the bevel on the cutting edge. The dimensions in the illustration will accommodate most gouges.

Cut the base and the guide from ½-inch plywood. Screw the guide together and fasten it to the base with screws countersunk from underneath. Make sure the opening created by the guide is large enough to allow the arm to slide through freely.

Cut the arm from 1-by-2 stock and the tool support from ½-inch plywood. Screw the two parts of the tool support together, then fasten

Tool Support
(back) ½" x 2" x 2 ¾"
(bottom) ½" x 1 ½" x 2 ¾"

Guide
(top) ½" x 1 ¾" x 9"
(sides) ½" x 1 ⅝" x 9"

Arm
¾" x 1 ½" x 25 ½"

V block
1 ½" x 1 ½" x 2 ¾"

Base
½" x 3" x 13 ½"

the bottom to the arm, flush with one end. For the V block, cut a small wood block to size and saw a 90° wedge out of one side. Glue the block to the tool support.

To use the jig, secure it to a work surface so the arm lines up directly under the grinding wheel. Seat the gouge handle in the V block and slide the arm so the beveled edge of the gouge sits flat on the grinding wheel. Clamp the arm in place. Then, with the gouge clear of the wheel, switch on the grinder and reposition the tool in the jig. Holding the gouge with both hands, rotate it from side-to-side so the beveled edge runs across the wheel *(left)*. Check the cutting edge periodically and stop grinding when the bevel forms.

DUST COLLECTION

A dust collection system has one aim: to capture most of the wood dust created at each of your woodworking machines and prevent it from ending up on the shop floor, or, worse yet, in the air. There are a series of variables in every system that must be coordinated to ensure a strong enough flow of air: the power of the collector; the location and requirements of the machines in the shop; and the type, size, and layout of the duct work.

The design of a central system begins with a simple bird's-eye view sketch of your shop, like the one shown below, arranging the machines and collector in their preferred locations. Then, draw in a main line running from the collector through the shop. Sketch in branch lines as needed to accommodate each machine and any obstructions—joists, beams, or fixtures—that may require special routing. For the best air flow, keep the main line and branch lines as short and straight as possible, and position the machines that produce the most dust closest to the collector. You may choose to run ducting along the ceiling of the shop, or, to increase the efficiency of the system, at machine-table height along the walls.

Since in most home shops only one woodworking machine will be producing dust at a time, 4- or 5-inch-diameter duct is sufficient for both the main and branch lines. There are several suitable types of duct available for dust collection systems. The best choice is metal duct designed specifically for dust collection. However, many woodworkers opt for plastic pipe, typically PVC or ABS. It is easier to seal and assemble (and disassemble for cleaning), less expensive, and more readily available.

Because plastic is an insulator, however, static build-up inside the pipe can reach dangerous levels during use—possibly high enough to ignite the dust passing through it. To prevent this, ground all plastic ducts by running a bare copper ground wire from each tool, inside the duct, to an electrical ground. As a safety precaution, have the system checked by an electrician. Smooth-wall rubber hose and flexible plastic hose, frequently used as branch ducts to connect machines to the main line, are other duct options for the home shop. Most of these products also require electrical grounding.

A central dust collection system requires a selection of fittings to route and join lengths of duct and dust hoods. The inventory on page 79 illustrates the elements of a typical dust collection system. If you run the main line along the ceiling, you can secure it in place with wire straps nailed to furring strips mounted between the joists.

Fittings directly affect the efficiency of the system, so choose them carefully. As a rule, gentle curves are better than sharp turns, so use Y fittings instead of

DESIGNING A SHOP FOR EFFICIENT DUST COLLECTION

Laying out a shop
The diagram at right illustrates a typical home shop layout. The power tools and dust collection system have been arranged for maximum dust collection efficiency. With the exception of the table saw, all the machines are situated on the perimeter of the work area. The ducting for the central dust collection system runs close to the walls. Despite requiring a relatively long main line, this design allows for short branch lines and minimal directional changes—both efficient arrangements. The space taken up by the dust collection system is minimized by placing the collector out of the way in a corner of the shop. The planer, probably the heaviest dust producer, is positioned closest to the collector to reduce strain on the system.

Ts for branch connections, wherever possible. A blast gate should be located at each branch outlet to seal ducts when they are not being used, thereby increasing air flow to the machine in use. Hoods, whether commercially made or shop-built, should be positioned as close as possible to the source of the dust.

You have a choice of methods for connecting ductwork. Many ducts and fittings can be friction fit and secured with adjustable hose clamps. Duct tape can also effectively join plastic pipe, but it is unsightly and will decay over time. A high-quality silicone sealant is probably a better choice for a permanent system. To ensure smooth air flow, metal ducts should be joined with rivets, rather than screws or bolts.

Once you have completed the layout of your system and selected the type of duct you will use, it is time to calculate your dust collection needs and select a collector. This involves determining the requirements of the heaviest dust collection task your system must handle. This usually will be the sum of system losses and the air volume demanded by the machine most distant from the collector. Purchase a collector with slightly more capacity. System losses are caused by such inefficiencies as bends in the line, corrugated ducting, leaks, and hoods without flanges. Use the charts and information on page 80 to size and select a collector.

ELEMENTS OF A DUST COLLECTION SYSTEM

Metal duct
Standard dust collection pipe; available in wide range of diameters

Reducer
Connects duct of different diameters; also used to increase suction in system or join a branch line to hood

Corrugated flexible hose
Ribbed plastic hose used for short runs or to connect machines to main duct; smooth-sided rubber or plastic varieties also available

Blast gate
Pipe fitting with sliding gate which is opened or closed to direct dust collection air flow to a particular machine

Splice
For joining two lengths of duct

Hose clamp
Slotted metal band and screw used to join two lengths of duct or hose

T connector
Connects two ducts at 90° angle

PVC pipe
Plastic pipe for small shop dust collection systems; available in different diameters and wall thicknesses

Hood
Dust-capturing device positioned close to source and connected to branch line

Elbow
Attaches to duct to change direction of line

Y connector
Joins two ducts at 30° or 45° angle

Adapters
Joins non-standard hose and duct to standard dust collection hose; also used to attach collection hose to factory-installed ports on stationary machines

Floor sweep
Attached to branch duct of central system to vacuum dust off shop floor

CALCULATING DUST COLLECTION NEEDS

Determining static pressure loss

Dust collectors are rated by their ability to move a certain number of cubic feet of air per minute (cfm) against a specific static pressure. The most important variable to keep in mind when choosing a dust collector for your shop is static pressure loss, which is a measure of the friction air encounters as it passes through a duct. The longer the ducting and the more numerous the system losses, the greater the static pressure loss. To determine the size of collector you need, calculate the static pressure loss for the heaviest collection task in the shop. In the diagram on page 78, it is the jointer. The following calculations are based on it. For your own shop, you may need to do the calculations for a few machines—those farthest from the collector and at the end of branch lines—and choose a collector based on the highest result you obtain.

Start with chart 1 *(right, top)* to calculate the equivalent length of the ducting running to the machine. In our example, there are 45 straight feet of smooth 4-inch-diameter duct and two 90° curved elbows. The equivalent length therefore is: 45 feet + 20 feet = 65 feet. Then use chart 2 *(middle)* to determine the exhaust requirements in cfm of the machine; for the jointer, it is 300 cfm.

Finally, use chart 3 *(bottom)* to determine static pressure loss for dust collection at the machine. Choose from either the third or fourth column of the chart depending on whether the machine is joined to a main-line duct (3500 feet per minute of air velocity, or fpm) or a branch line (4000 fpm). In this example, a 300-cfm machine connected to a 4-inch-diameter main line has a static pressure loss of .05 inches per foot. Thus the static pressure loss for this jointer is: 65 feet x .05 inches/foot = 3.25 inches. Add two inches for unmeasured losses like air leaks and the value rises to 5.25 inches. The shop on page 78 would need a collector with a 300 cfm rating at 5.25 inches of static pressure. A system 20 percent larger would allow for future expansion.

(1) EQUIVALENT LENGTH OF SYSTEM ELEMENTS

Duct or Fitting	Equivalent Length, in Feet
Smooth-wall pipe	Actual length
Corrugated pipe or hose	1.5 x actual length
Unflanged duct, hose, or hood connections	10
90° sharp elbow	20
90° curved elbow	10
90° hose bend	10
45° curved elbow	5
45° hose bend	5
Side leg of 90° T	20
Side leg of 45° Y	5

(2) AIR EXHAUST VOLUME REQUIREMENTS FOR MACHINES

Machine	Cubic Feet per Minute (CFM)
Jointer (4-12")	300
Disc sander (up to 12")	300
Vertical belt sander (up to 6")	350
Band saw (up to 2" blade)	400
Table saw (up to 16")	300
Radial arm saw	350
Planer (up to 20")	400
Shaper (½" spindle)	300
Shaper (1" spindle)	500
Lathe	500
Floor sweep	350
Drill press	300
Jig saw	300

(3) STATIC PRESSURE LOSS PER FOOT OF DUCT AT 3500 AND 4000 FPM

CFM	Duct diameter	3500 fpm	4000 fpm
300	4"	.05 in/ft	.07 in/ft
350	4"	.05 in/ft	.07 in/ft
400	4"	.05 in/ft	.06 in/ft
500	5"	.04 in/ft	.06 in/ft

DUST COLLECTORS

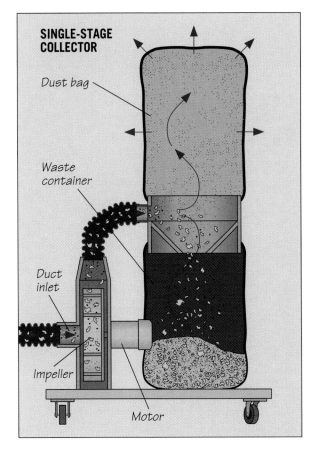

SINGLE-STAGE COLLECTOR

Dust bag

Waste container

Duct inlet

Impeller

Motor

TWO-STAGE COLLECTOR

Motor

Impeller

Duct inlet

Dust bag

Waste container

SHOP TIP

Electrical sweeps for right-angle joints

If you use PVC pipe for your dust collection system, substitute 90° electrical sweeps *(far right)* for conventional 90° elbows *(near right)* to reduce friction and increase the efficiency of your system. Available at electrical supply houses, these fittings feature a 24-inch radius curve, which is much gentler than the 5- to 10-inch radius curve of standard elbows.

Choosing between single- and two-stage collectors

Two basic types of dust collectors are available for home workshops: single- and two-stage machines. In single-stage collectors *(above, left)*, debris- and dust-laden air is drawn through an impeller, where cyclone action deposits heavy dust and debris into the waste container below while the lighter dust rises to the dust bag. Single-stage collectors are relatively loud and the dust and debris tend to wear out the bag and impeller quickly. In two-stage collectors *(above, right)*, the impeller is located above the inlet duct so the heavier particles drop into the waste container before any air passes through the impeller and bag. This is quieter, and reduces wear on the impeller and dust bag. Two-stage collectors are somewhat more difficult to clean.

DUST HOODS

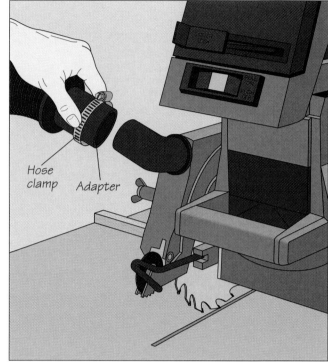

Connecting a dust collection system to tools with dust ports

Use a commercial adapter to attach a collection hose to a machine dust port. The adapter should be sized to friction-fit with the collection hose at one end and slip over the dust port at the other, as shown on the band saw *(above, left)*. For the radial arm saw, a hose clamp is used for reinforcement *(above, right)*.

Hooking a planer up to the system

A hood like the one shown at right can be custom-built to capture most of the dust generated by your planer. Make the hood from galvanized sheet metal, cutting the pieces with tin snips. Leave tabs where the pieces overlap so they can be pop riveted together. Make flanges on the sides to improve the seal and a hole in the back for the dust collection hose; you will also need to create a lip along the top to connect to the ledge of the planer's chip discharge chute. Use an adapter to join the hood to the hose, inserting one end in the hole in the hood and the other end in the hose; reinforce the connection with a hose clamp. Fasten the lip of the hood to the planer with sheet metal screws.

Top
flange

Angle
iron

Support
bracket

Back
flange

Collection hose

SHOP TIP

Adapting standard sheet-metal ducts as dust hoods

Commercial sheet-metal ducts can be modified to serve as efficient hoods for your shop's dust collection system. Some examples are shown here. Use tin snips to cut the duct to a shape that suits the tool at hand. The duct should fit snugly around the chip discharge port or dust spout of the machine. Screw it in place with sheet metal screws.

Connecting a collection hood to a router table

A hood attached to the fence of a router table will collect most of the dust produced by the tool. Cut the hood from $\frac{1}{2}$-inch plywood, sizing it so the sides hug the outside edges of the fence's support brackets. The bottom edge of the back flange should rest on the table; the top flange should sit on the top edge of the fence. Before assembling the pieces of the hood, cut a hole through the back for the collection hose. Also bore holes for screws through the sides and screw angle irons to the back so that their inside edges are flush with the opening for the hose. Screw the hood together, then fit the collection hose in the back. Use a hose clamp to secure the hose to the angle irons and position the hood on the fence (above). Screw the sides of the hood to the fence brackets.

Collection outlet

Setting up a shop-made sanding station
To reduce the amount of dust generated by power sanding, build a portable stall that fits on a table or workbench. Cut the back, top, and sides from ½- or ¾-inch plywood. Taper the top edges of the sides to create a comfortable, open working space, like the one shown above. Cut an outlet in the back of the station for a dust collection hose or branch duct. Assemble the station with screws. Position the sanding station securely on your work surface; attach the collector hose to the outlet. Turn on the collector before you begin a sanding operation.

SHOP TIP

Shop-made blast gate
To fashion an inexpensive blast gate for a plastic duct, saw halfway through the pipe. Cut a gate from plywood or hardboard to fit in the kerf. Saw a semicircle in one half of the gate the same size as the inside diameter of the pipe; the other half should protrude from the kerf to form a handle. To seal the slot when the machine is in use, cut a sleeve from the same size of pipe with a diagonal slit to allow it to slide over the kerf.

PORTABLE DUST COLLECTION

A central dust collection system may sound like overkill to the craftsman with a small home shop. Although such systems are generally more efficient than independent collectors, they can be costly and consume considerable space. If your shop area is restricted, and only one machine will be operated at a time, consider a portable dust collector.

Many types of portable dust collectors are available. Most are strong enough to power a central system, yet light enough to be toted around the shop. If you are planning to set up a portable collection system, shop around for the most transportable collector that can handle your needs. Keep in mind that you may want to expand to a central system later.

Many home woodworkers will find that a shop vacuum, although not ideal, can do a satisfactory job most of the time if you are willing to work around the

Although you can hook up a band saw to a central dust collection system, another solution is to attach it to a portable shop vacuum. The vacuum's hose can often be slipped around an existing port on the machine using a simple commercial reducer.

drawbacks. Shop vacuums are designed to move a small volume of air at high velocity through a small-diameter hose. Dust collectors, on the other hand, move a large amount of air at a lower speed. A shop vacuum dust hood, therefore, should be positioned very close to the tool. Larger chips will tend to clog vacuum hoses, requiring frequent cleaning. And, vacuums powered by universal motors tend to wear out quickly. Models with induction-type electric motors will last longer, but cost more than a portable dust collector of the same power.

If there is no dust collection system—portable or central—in your shop, try the methods described starting on page 86 to control airborne dust. These methods are also effective supplements to collectors that suck up a majority of shop dust, but still leave some particles floating in the air.

AN AUXILIARY PORTABLE DUST COLLECTION SYSTEM

Exhaust port

Dust collection hose

Intake port

90° elbow

Shop vacuum

55-gallon drum

Expanding a dust collector's capacity

You can more than double the capacity of your portable dust collector or shop vacuum by attaching a 55-gallon drum or a large plastic barrel as a mid-stage collector. Install plastic intake and exhaust ports on the drum as shown at left and mount a hose to the intake port on the drum to collect wood dust and chips. The 90° elbow on the intake port will create a cyclone effect inside the barrel, forcing chips and heavier sawdust against the walls of the barrel. Lighter dust will be drawn through the exhaust port into the shop vacuum or dust collector. For easy assembly and disassembly, use pipe fittings that form a friction fit with the hose from your vacuum or collector.

CONTROLLING AIRBORNE DUST

Setting up positive-pressure ventilation

To maintain clear air in a shop when you are generating a great deal of airborne dust or chemical fumes, set up a positive-pressure ventilation (PPV) system. Open all the windows in the shop and position a fan outside the door as shown at right so that the airflow it produces will envelop the doorway. The stream of air will follow the path of least resistance—through the door and shop, and out the windows, clearing airborne dust and fumes quickly. PPV has some limitations, however. The system will only function properly if the window openings are large enough to handle a sufficient volume of air. Also, the rest of your home must be well sealed off from the shop. A more permanent alternative to PPV can be fashioned by mounting an explosion-proof exhaust fan in a shop window. Set up to pull air out of the room, the fan will create negative pressure, expelling fumes and dust in larger volumes than is possible with PPV.

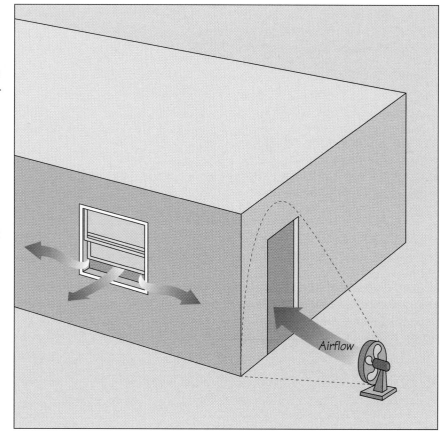

Airflow

SHOP TIP

Vacuum screening ramp

For cleaning dust off the shop floor, build a wedge-shaped screening ramp from ½-inch plywood. Before assembling the pieces, cut an inlet port in the back to fit a dust collection hose and five rows of 2-inch-diameter holes through the top. When dust and chips are swept up onto the ramp, smaller particles will fall through the holes and continue on to the collector. Larger refuse will remain on the ramp for easy disposal.

Furnace filter

Filtering shop air

Another quick and easy method of ridding the shop of airborne dust uses a furnace filter on the back of a portable room fan *(above)*. When the fan is turned on, suction will hold the filter in place and draw dust out of the air. The dust will remain on the filter, which can then be brushed off outside or vacuumed.

SHOP TIP

Panty hose shop vacuum filter
Used panty hose can serve as an inexpensive alternative to replaceable shop vacuum dust filters. Fit the waist band around the foam filter sleeve on the underside of the motor housing of the vacuum and knot the legs. Slide the retaining ring around the panty hose to secure it in place.

STORAGE

Flammable products like lacquers, shellacs, and paint thinners require special attention. Storing these items in a double-lined, explosion-proof steel cabinet is one sensible solution.

Clutter is the woodworker's enduring enemy. Whether your workshop is shoehorned into the corner of the basement or spread out in a two-car garage, it no doubt accumulates things at an astonishing rate: Lumber, plywood, saws, saw blades, drills, drill bits, planes, clamps, chisels, files, grinders, screwdrivers, punches, wrenches, and hammers are just a few of the hand and power tools that must be conveniently available when needed—and out of the way when not.

Add to these the lumber scraps, locks, hinges, screws, nails, spare parts, and containers half full of finishes—all sure to be invaluable some day very soon—and you may have the makings of a monumental storage problem.

Adequate workshop storage should accomplish two goals: Tools and materials should be kept within easy reach of each operation, and the storage devices should encroach as little as possible on work space. No matter what your particular needs, you should find a number of storage ideas that conserve space in this chapter.

In evaluating your own storage options begin by taking two inventories: one of your tools and materials and the other of unused space—corners, spaces under the stairs, between wall studs, below the workbench, and between the ceiling joists. Lumber and plywood are best stored on racks that prevent warping and water damage, keeping the wood out of the way and easy to reach. Shelves, drawers, and cabinets are the most convenient and economical spaces for storing tools. There are a variety of commercial storage devices on the market, but you can build a tool cabinet customized to your needs easily and inexpensively *(page 96)*. The design shown on page 98 fulfills two needs in one: a storage cabinet that folds down and serves as a sturdy work surface. Hardware can be sorted in drawers, subdivided into separate compartments or, for greater visibility, in glass containers. For tools like clamps that are used all over the shop, consider a wheeled rack *(page 105)*.

No matter what devices and techniques you choose, you may find that proper storage not only provides more space and convenience, but conveys a sense of order and purpose that will make your shop an even more pleasant and productive place to work.

Whatever its size, a tool chest can serve as a cabinetmaker's calling card. This portable carver's chest keeps tools organized, safe from damage, and within easy reach.

STORING WOOD

P roperly stored lumber and plywood are not only kept out of the way but straight and dry, too. For most shops, this involves storing lumber in racks that hold the wood off the floor. Wood shrinks and expands according to the amount of humidity to which it is exposed. A wet floor can warp lumber and delaminate some plywoods. The lumber racks featured in this section are easy and inexpensive to build; you should be able to find a suitable design and adapt it to your needs.

If you have the space, you can set up an end-loading lumber rack like the one shown on page 91. Such a system is relatively easy to construct but you will need a wall twice the length of your lumber to allow for loading and unloading. If space in your shop is at a premium, consider a front-loading rack like the one shown below. If versatility is needed, examine

the rack on page 92, which allows you to store boards both horizontally and vertically. Avoid using Z-shaped brackets; they waste too much space.

The typical shop can stock hundreds of pounds of lumber, so it is crucial to anchor your rack firmly—to at least every second wall stud or floor joist.

Make the most of spaces that you would not ordinarily consider as prime storage areas. If your ceiling is unfinished, nail furring strips across the joists for handy shelving to store short stock and dowels.

Every item in a workshop demands its own storage method. The dowel rack at left, built from ³⁄₄-inch plywood, 1-by-4 stock and 6-inch-diameter cardboard tubes, sorts different sizes of dowels while taking up a minimum of floor space.

A LUMBER RACK

Storing planks and boards

The storage rack at right features vertical supports screwed to wall studs. Cut from 2-by-4 stock, the supports buttress shop-made wood brackets, which hold up the lumber. You will need one support at each end of the rack, with an additional one every 32 inches along the wall. After bolting the supports to the studs, prepare the brackets by cutting the sides from ³⁄₄-inch plywood and the middle shelf piece from 2-by-4 stock 1½ inches shorter than the brackets. Angle the top edge of the sides by about 5° so the brackets will tilt up slightly *(inset)* and prevent the lumber from falling off the rack. Screw the middle shelf piece to the sides, then screw the bracket to the vertical supports.

Shelf

Bracket

Vertical support

BUILD IT YOURSELF

A LUMBER-AND-PLYWOOD RACK
Designed to accommodate both boards and plywood panels, the rack shown rests on the shop floor and attaches to joists in the ceiling. Lumber is loaded onto the rails from the end, while plywood can be stacked in the trough at the front and held in place by the hinged bar. Refer to the cutting list for suggested dimensions.

To build the rack, first cut the rails and stiles from 2-by-4 stock, then notch them together *(inset)*: Starting 24 inches from the bottom end of the stiles, cut a series of 3½-inch-wide, 1½-inch-deep dadoes every 24 inches. Cut rabbets at both ends of each rail to match the dadoes in the stiles. Screw the rails and stiles together, then bolt the top ends of the stiles to every third joist, making them 48

inches apart. Once the grid is fixed to the ceiling joists, screw the crossbars to the front stiles, centering them between the rails.

Assemble the plywood trough with screws before fastening it to the bottom of the front stiles. Finally, attach the hinged bar to the trough lip with a butt hinge, and cut two notches in the free end of the bar for a looped cord to hold the bar upright.

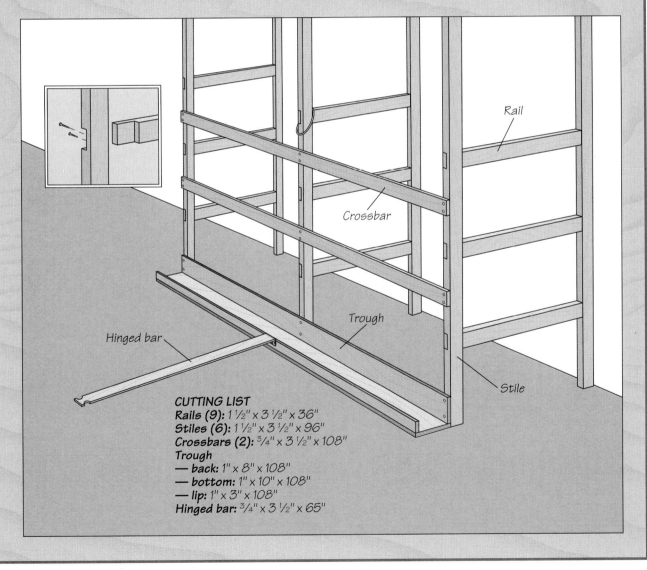

Rail

Crossbar

Trough

Hinged bar

Stile

CUTTING LIST
Rails (9): 1½" x 3½" x 36"
Stiles (6): 1½" x 3½" x 96"
Crossbars (2): ¾" x 3½" x 108"
Trough
— *back:* 1" x 8" x 108"
— *bottom:* 1" x 10" x 108"
— *lip:* 1" x 3" x 108"
Hinged bar: ¾" x 3½" x 65"

ADJUSTABLE LUMBER RACKS

Upright

Steel pipe

Crosspiece

Dado joint

Pipe angle

Building an adjustable pipe rack

The rack shown above, made of 4-by-4 stock and steel pipe, is attached to wall studs. The steel pipes should be roughly 24 inches long and ¾ inch in diameter. They can be inserted into any of the holes drilled into the vertical supports or crosspieces, allowing lumber to be piled on the pipes or stacked on end between them. Begin by cutting the uprights to length and mark each point on them where you want to locate a crosspiece. Cut dadoes in the sides of the uprights to accommodate the crosspieces *(inset)*, making sure all the crosspieces in the same horizontal row will be at the same level. Bore holes into the uprights and crosspieces for the pipes; drill the holes 3 inches deep and 6 inches apart, angling them by about 5° so the pipes will tilt up slightly. Bolt the uprights to the studs, then cut the crosspieces to length and tap them in between the uprights with a mallet. Fix them in place with glue or by driving in screws at an angle.

Bracket

Strapping

SHOP TIP

Anchoring lumber racks in concrete
Since ordinary wood or sheet metal screws do not hold well in concrete, you will need different fasteners than you would use for wood. Lead anchors (top) combined with lag bolts are ideal for anchoring to concrete. Inserted into a hole drilled in the concrete, the anchor expands as the bolt is driven into it, gripping the sides of the hole tightly. Another option is the self-tapping concrete screw (bottom). Its serrated threads hold fast in concrete.

Setting up adjustable lumber shelves
A commercial lumber storage system like the one shown above consists of metal strapping and brackets that fit into holes in the strapping. The rack is similar to the wooden one on page 90, but because it is metal, this rack can typically support heavier loads. Bolt the strapping directly to the wall studs, or to vertical supports fastened to non-exposed studs. Make sure the straps are aligned laterally to allow you to position each row of brackets at the same height. For most applications, attach the brackets to the strapping about 24 to 36 inches apart vertically.

STORING TOOLS AND SUPPLIES

Shelves are an ideal tool storage option. This shop-built unit features grooves and cleats custom-cut to hang a panoply of tools in full view over a workbench.

"A place for everything and everything in its place." That time-worn adage is especially appropriate for the home workshop. From shelves and racks to tool chests and partitioned drawers, many devices will eliminate clutter while keeping tools and supplies easily accessible. A few methods are shown in the following pages.

For certain tools, particularly items that are valuable or dangerous enough to be out of the reach of children, wall-mounted boxes like those shown below are ideal. For a more traditional system of enclosed storage, you can build a tool cabinet or cupboard in the shop *(page 96)*. But not every storage device needs to be elaborate. As shown on page 101, suspending a tool from a fastener driven into a wall can work just fine.

WALL STORAGE

Installing portable cabinets

The box at right can be hung securely on a shop wall and easily moved if necessary. Build it from ¾-inch plywood with a hinged top. To hang the cabinet on the wall, cut a 45° angle bevel down the middle of a 1-by-6, then crosscut the two pieces slightly less than the width of the box. Screw one of the pieces to the wall as a batten, with the bevel pointing up and facing the wall; anchor as many of the fasteners as possible in wall studs. Screw the other piece to the back of the box with its flat edge butting against the lip and the bevel pointing down and facing the back. The two pieces interlock when the box is hung on the wall *(inset)*.

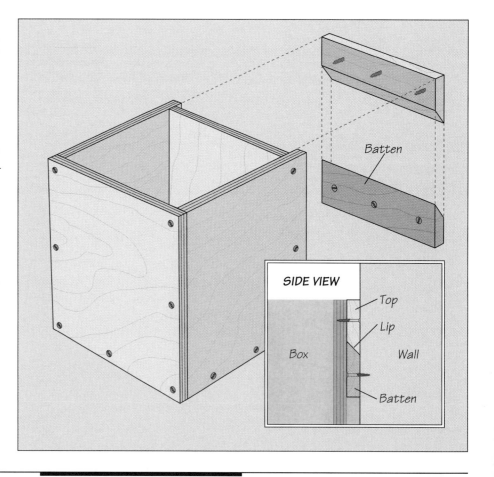

Batten

SIDE VIEW

Top
Lip
Box
Wall
Batten

Building shelves for tools and supplies

The shelving shown above can be fastened to a concrete foundation wall using lead anchors or concrete screws *(page 93)*. If your shop has a stud wall, anchor the uprights to the studs. Begin by cutting the uprights from 1-by-4 stock, allowing 32 inches of space between the uprights in order to fasten them to studs. To add a shelf, cut a brace from 1-by-2 stock and make a triangular bracket for every upright. Saw the brackets so that the side facing up is about 2 inches shorter than the width of the shelf. Also cut notches in the brackets for the brace, then screw them to the uprights, making sure they are all at the same height. To hang tools from the unit, screw a 1-by-6 across the uprights, then bore holes into the board for 1-inch-diameter dowel pegs. Glue the dowels in the holes.

BUILD IT YOURSELF

Leather saw strap

Divider

A TOOL CABINET

The tool cabinet shown above is handy for storing and organizing hand tools. Although the entire unit is portable, the drawers are removable, making it possible to carry around only the tools that are needed. Build the cabinet from either ³⁄₄-inch plywood or solid lumber. The size of the box will depend on your needs but 40 inches high by 30 inches wide by 15 inches deep is a good starting point. Position the divider in the center of the cabinet so that the spaces on both sides of it are equal, making the drawers interchangeable.

Cut the pieces to size, then prepare the sides of the cabinet and the divider for the drawers: Rout a series of ¹⁄₄-by-¹⁄₄-inch dadoes on one face of the sides and on both faces of the divider. Make the space between the dadoes equal to the height of the drawers, plus ¹⁄₄-inch for clearance. Glue up the cabinet, shelf, divider, and door, using the joint of your choice. The cabinet in the illustration was assembled with plate, or biscuit, joints. Nail a leather strap to the inside of the door for hanging tools, add a wood strip to prevent small items from falling out, then attach the door to the cabinet with butt hinges.

Next, build the drawers. Saw the pieces to size, using ¹⁄₄-inch plywood for the bottom; orient the panels so the grain of the face veneer runs from the front of the drawer to the back. Cut the sides slightly shorter than the depth of the cabinet if you are working with lumber, to allow for wood movement. Make the drawer front ¹⁄₄-inch wider and cut a rabbet along its bottom edge to conceal the bottom, and notch the top edge for a handle. Cut dadoes in the sides for dividers. Glue up the drawers; the bottoms should extend beyond both sides by ¹⁄₄ inch to form sliders that fit in the cabinet dadoes.

BUILD IT YOURSELF

Ledge

Slotted shelf

Cleat

Door ledge

Shelf divider

A TOOL CUPBOARD

The cupboard above features twin doors for storing small, light tools like chisels and screwdrivers, as well as a large main compartment for bigger tools. Cut the components from ¾-inch plywood or lumber to the appropriate size, depending on the number of tools you own; the cupboard shown above is 48 inches square and 5 inches deep with 3-inch-deep doors. Next, assemble the cupboard using the joinery method of your choice. A through dovetail joint is one of the strongest and most visually pleasing

options. But you could choose a method as simple as counterbored screws concealed under wood plugs, as shown above.

To help you install the shelves, lay the cupboard on its back and place the tools to be stored in their designated spots. Position the shelves accordingly and screw them in place. To keep supplies from rolling off a shelf or the bottom of the doors, glue a ledge along the front edge. If you want to subdivide a shelf, screw 1-by-1 cleats across it or install vertical dividers between

the shelves.

Equip one or both doors with slotted shelves to hold tools like chisels and screwdrivers. Bore a series of holes slightly smaller than the tool handles, then saw a kerf from the edge of the shelf to the hole to enable you to slip in the blade. Screw the shelves to the door.

Hang the doors on the cupboard with butt or piano hinges. Use three butt hinges per door. Mount the cupboard to the wall above your workbench, if desired, by screwing it to the wall studs.

BUILD IT YOURSELF

A FOLD-DOWN WORKBENCH AND TOOL CABINET

Ideal for small workshops, the storage cabinet shown below and opposite features a door that serves double-duty as a sturdy work surface that folds up out of the way when it is not needed. Mounted on a frame that is anchored to wall studs, the unit is built with an adjustable shelf and a perforated hardboard back for organizing and hanging tools as well as a work table supported by folding legs. The cabinet-bench can be made entirely of ¾-inch plywood, except for the legs and leg rail, which are cut from 2-by-4 stock; the 1-by-3 frame; the 1-by-4 hinge brace assembly; and the hardboard back.

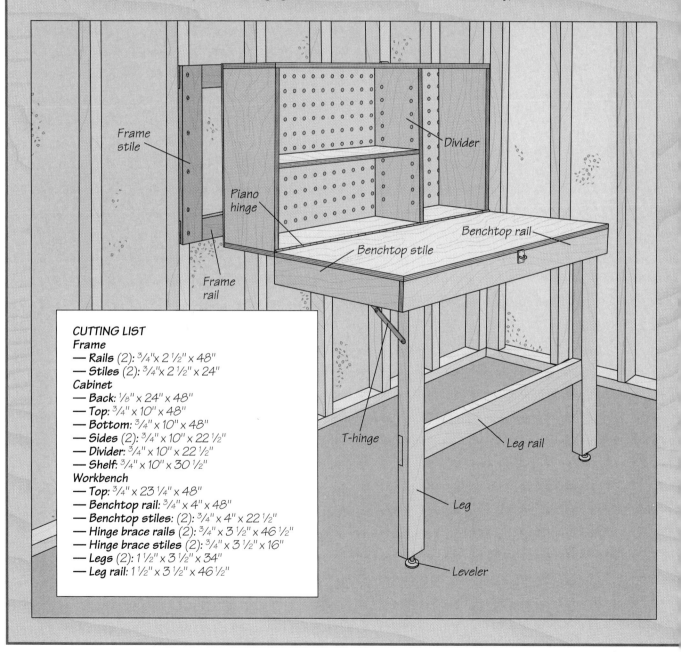

CUTTING LIST
Frame
— *Rails* (2): ¾"x 2 ½" x 48"
— *Stiles* (2): ¾"x 2 ½" x 24"
Cabinet
— *Back:* ⅛" x 24" x 48"
— *Top:* ¾" x 10" x 48"
— *Bottom:* ¾" x 10" x 48"
— *Sides* (2): ¾" x 10" x 22 ½"
— *Divider:* ¾" x 10" x 22 ½"
— *Shelf:* ¾" x 10" x 30 ½"
Workbench
— *Top:* ¾" x 23 ¼" x 48"
— *Benchtop rail:* ¾" x 4" x 48"
— *Benchtop stiles:* (2): ¾" x 4" x 22 ½"
— *Hinge brace rails* (2): ¾" x 3 ½" x 46 ½"
— *Hinge brace stiles* (2): ¾" x 3 ½" x 16"
— *Legs* (2): 1 ½" x 3 ½" x 34"
— *Leg rail:* 1 ½" x 3 ½" x 46 ½"

Labels: Frame stile, Divider, Piano hinge, Benchtop rail, Benchtop stile, Frame rail, T-hinge, Leg rail, Leg, Leveler

Build the unit in three steps, starting with the frame, then making the cabinet section, and finally cutting and attaching the work table and legs. Referring to the cutting list for suggested dimensions, cut rabbets in the frame rails and stiles, then glue and screw them together. Next, screw the frame to the studs in your shop. Be sure to position the frame so that the work surface will be at a comfortable height, typically about 36 inches off the floor. Now build the cabinet section, cutting the parts to size. Before assembling the pieces, bore two parallel rows of holes on the inside face of one side panel and the opposing face of the divider. Drill the holes at 1-inch intervals about 2 inches in from the edges of the panels. By inserting commercially available shelf supports in the holes, the height of the shelf can be adjusted to suit your particular needs. With the exception of the shelf, screw the parts together, then cut the hardboard to size and nail it to the cabinet. Fit the unit against the frame and use screws to attach the cabinet to the frame.

Saw the parts of the workbench to size, then screw the hinge brace rails and stiles and the benchtop rail and stiles to the underside of the bench-top *(above, right)*. Attach the bench-top to the bottom of the cabinet section with a piano hinge, making sure the two edges are perfectly aligned.

With the workbench folded down and held parallel to the floor, measure the distance from the hinge brace rail to the floor and cut the legs to fit. Attach the legs to the rail with hinges, then screw levelers to the bottom of the legs and adjust them as necessary to level the bench-top. Add a folding metal brace to each leg for added support, screwing the flat end of the brace to the hinge brace stile and the other end to the outside edge of the leg. Also cut a leg rail to fit between the legs and screw it in place. Finally, install a hasp lock, screwing one part to the top of the cabinet and the other part to the benchtop rail.

STORING SAWS AND BLADES

Building a handsaw storage rack

The handsaw storage rack shown at right saves space by storing saws upright. The blades fit in kerfs cut in the brackets and the handles rest on notches cut in the front; the dividers prevent the saws from contacting each other. Start by cutting the sides, top, bottom, and back from $\frac{3}{4}$-inch plywood, sizing the pieces to accommodate the length and number of your saws. Rout dadoes at $1\frac{1}{2}$-inch intervals in the back and bottom for the dividers, then screw the five pieces together, making sure the dadoes in the back and bottom align. Using $\frac{3}{4}$-inch-thick solid lumber for the front and brackets, saw the front piece to length, but leave it a few inches wider than you need. Then cut a series of dadoes in the front that line up with those in the bottom and back. To create the notches in the front for the saw handles, bore a row of $\frac{3}{4}$-inch-diameter holes through it close to the top edge between the dadoes. Next, cut along the length of the front through the center of the holes, leaving semicircular notches. Cut the dividers from $\frac{1}{4}$-inch plywood and slip them into place in the back and bottom. Install the front, screwing it to the sides. Next, cut the brackets to fit between the sides and saw $\frac{1}{8}$-inch-wide kerfs across their edges, taking care to center them over the spaces between the dividers. Chamfer the mouth of each kerf to make it easier to slip the blades into the rack. Screw the brackets to the back and sides and mount the rack on a wall if you wish. To avoid nicking yourself on a blade, always place saws in the rack with the teeth facing the back.

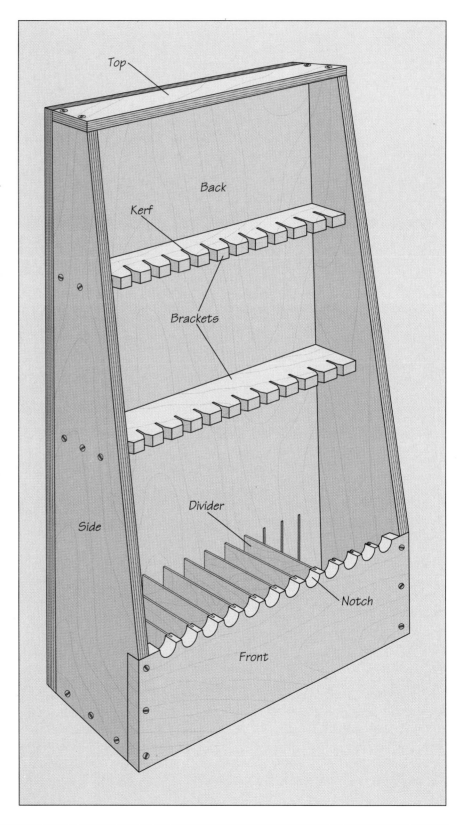

BUILD IT YOURSELF

A HANDSAW HOLDER

Build a wall-mounted rack for handsaws with a few wood scraps, doweling, and some rubber hose. Cut the base from ½-inch plywood and the dividers from 4-by-4 stock; the dividers should be 10 inches long. Cut a taper at the end of each 4-by-4, as shown at right. Screw a 2-by-4 along one edge of the base, then screw the dividers in place, leaving a ½-inch gap between them. The stoppers are cut from 4-inch lengths of ½-inch dowel and slightly larger rubber hose; use hose with ridges rather than smooth garden hose. Slip a saw into the rack from below, then tug down on the handle. The stopper will pinch the blade in place. Mark the dowel's position and screw it to the base.

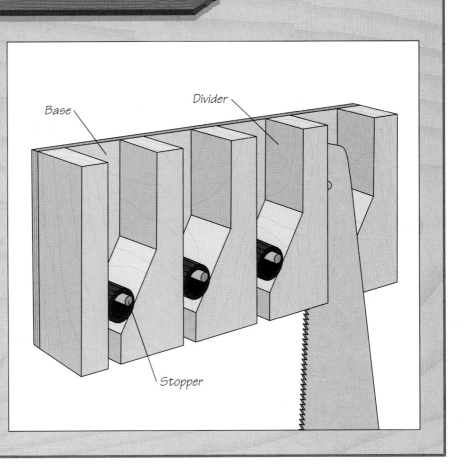

Base

Divider

Stopper

SHOP TIP

Hanging portable power tools from the wall
A simple but easily overlooked solution to the problem of storing tools where they can be seen is to hang them from the shop wall. Drive a nail, screw, or threaded eye hook into the wall, making sure it is anchored to a stud. Loop a length of nylon rope around the tool handle, then hang the rope from the fastener. Leave the rope hanging from the wall when you are using the tool as a reminder to return it to its rightful place when you are finished.

Divider

Batten

Organizing circular saw blades

Keep your circular saw blades visible and protected in a custom-made storage box like the one above. Build the box from ½-inch plywood, cutting it a few inches larger than your largest blade and wide enough to hold all your blades. Make the dividers out of ¼-inch plywood; first cut rectangles 1 inch less than the size of the sides, then saw them in half diagonally. Screw the frame together, then glue and nail the dividers to the bottom and back. Leave ¼ inch between the dividers. To keep the blades from rolling out of the box, cut a batten from scrap stock and nail it to the dividers near the bottom of the box.

SHOP TIP

A circular saw blade carrier
To avoid damaging your circular saw blades, or nicking yourself when the blades are being stored or transported, use a commercial blade carrier. The model shown accommodates up to 10 blades, protecting the cutting edges with a plastic rim while leaving the blades visible. When storing several blades at once, separate them with cardboard spacers to prevent the teeth from making contact.

KEEPING TOOLS ORGANIZED

2" x 4"
attached
to joist

Wedge

Divider

Tool tray

Notched
2" x 4"

Adding tool-tray dividers

To protect tool edges in storage drawers, saw a 2-by-4 to a length equal to the space between the drawer sides. Then cut dadoes across one side of the board to hold the tools—in this case, narrow dadoes to accommodate file blades *(above)*.

Storing hand tools

The tool tray shown above keeps different tools apart and similar ones together, helping to protect them while making a needed item easy to locate. The tray has the additional advantage of being suspended from overhead joists so that it takes up no valuable work space. Start by bolting two 2-by-4s to joists, spacing them to accommodate the tray. Cut off the bottom ends of the 2-by-4s at a convenient height. Next, build the tray, cutting the sides from ½-inch stock, and the bottom and the dividers from ¼-inch plywood. Cut dadoes for the dividers according to how you wish to group your tools, then screw the sides together and to the bottom. Glue the dividers in the dadoes and screw the sides to the 2-by-4s. Screw the back to wall studs, or, using lead anchors, to a concrete wall. If you plan to install the tray at an angle, as shown, drive the screws through wood wedges placed between the tray and the wall.

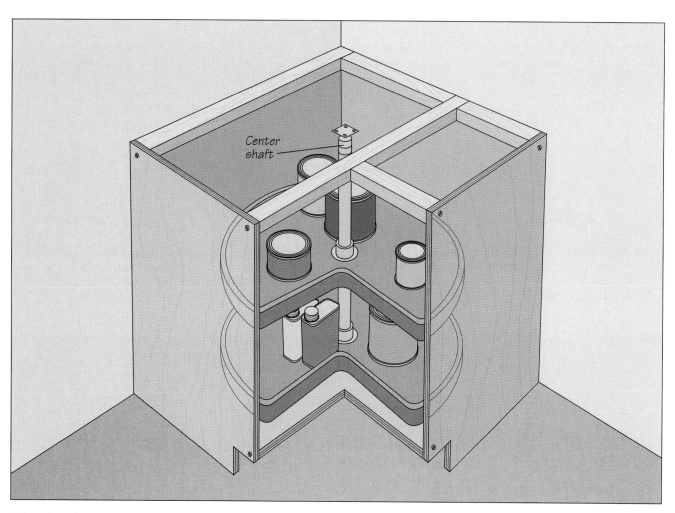

Center shaft

Using a Lazy Susan-type storage cupboard
If your workshop has an unused corner —an area under a counter, for example, install a commercial Lazy Susan-type cupboard to store workshop tools and supplies. The design of the device makes any item on the trays easily accessible. The model shown above features a carousel with two trays that revolve around a metal shaft. Using ¾-inch plywood, build a cabinet like the one shown above to house the carousel and support the metal shaft at both the top and bottom. Assemble the carousel following the manufacturer's instructions.

SHOP TIP

A magnetic tool rack
Keep metal tools organized and accessible on a commercial magnetic tool rack. The model shown features a heavy-duty bar magnet that will hold any iron-based tool securely—from screwdrivers, chisels, and hammers to try squares and scissors. To mount the rack, screw the magnet to a wood strip and anchor the strip to wall studs above your workbench.

BUILD IT YOURSELF

A MOBILE CLAMP RACK

Clamps can be a nuisance to store. The sheer number accumulated in most shops—and their awkward size and shape—can stretch even the most organized storage system to the limit. The mobile clamp rack shown below stores a wide variety of clamps. With casters mounted under the base, the rack can be rolled to any part of the shop where clamps are needed, then stored against the wall.

Refer to the cutting list for suggested dimensions.

Start by cutting the rails, stiles, and crosspieces to size from 2-by-4 stock. Then join the pieces together using lap joints and notches. To prepare the rails for the joinery, rout end rabbets that will fit into the notches and dadoes cut into the stiles. The rabbets should be 1½ inches wide and ¾ inch deep. Next, notch the top end of each stile on three sides as shown, then rout back-to-back dadoes near the bottom end and middle of the stiles; make the dadoes 3½ inches wide and ¾ inch deep. Also cut a notch 3½ inches wide and ¾ inch deep from the bottom of each stile.

When you assemble the rails and stiles, align the two halves of each rail face-to-face and assemble with the stile. Screw the pieces together, driving the fasteners through the joints.

To join the crosspieces to the rack, cut 3½-inch-wide dadoes in the middle of each and screw them in place. The middle crosspieces will rest on the median rail. The top pieces will rest on the outside shoulders of the notched top of each stile.

Finish the rack by cutting the four pieces for the skirt from 2-by-4 stock and the base from ¼-inch plywood. Saw two notches in the base and skirt to accommodate the stiles, rabbet the ends of the skirt pieces, and screw them together to form a box. Use screws to attach the skirt to the base. Finally, attach casters to the underside of the skirt at each corner of the rack and fasten the base to the stiles and bottom rail, driving the screws from underneath the base.

CUTTING LIST
—*Rails (top, bottom, and median) (6):* 1¾" x 3½" x 23½"
—*Stiles (2):* 1½" x 3½" x 44½"
—*Crosspieces (3):* 1½" x 3½" x 23½"
—*Base:* ¼" x 23½" x 23½"
—*Skirt pieces (4):* ½" x 3½" x 23½"

Top rail

Stile

Crosspiece

Median rail

Bottom rail

Base

Caster

Skirt

A SHELF FOR CLAMPS

Built from ½-inch plywood, the shelf shown at right features a series of notches for supporting bar and pipe clamps along a shop wall. Cut the shelf about 10 inches wide and as long as you need for the number of clamps you wish to store. Cut the notches at 3-inch intervals with a saber saw and make them wide enough for the clamp bars or pipes; 1¼ inches is about right for most clamps. Then screw shelf brackets to the underside of the shelf, centering them between the notches. Fasten the shelf to a backing board of ½-inch plywood, then anchor the board to the wall studs.

Backing board

Shelf

Shelf bracket

SHOP TIP

Storing clamps in a can

A trash can fitted with a shop-made lid serves as a convenient way to store small bar or pipe clamps. Cut a piece of ½-inch plywood into a circle slightly smaller than the diameter of the can's rim. Then scribe a series of concentric circles on the plywood to help you locate the holes for the clamp bars. Space the circles about 3 inches apart and mark points every 3 inches along them. Bore a 1-inch-diameter hole through each point, fit the piece of plywood in the can and drop the clamps through the holes.

TWO WALL RACKS FOR CLAMPS

Plywood strip

Broom gripper

Cleat

Cleat

Base

Making and installing the racks

Shop walls make ideal storage areas for bar and pipe clamps. For bar clamps *(above, left)*, nail two cleats across the wall studs. Position the upper cleat—made of plywood—high enough to keep the clamps off the floor; make the lower one from two 2-by-4s nailed together so that the clamps will tilt toward the wall. For pipe clamps *(above, right)*, nail cleats of ¾-inch plywood to the studs and screw broom grippers to the cleats. Position the cleats on the wall so the clamps will rest about 1 inch off the floor. Then cut the base from 1-by-4 stock, and bore a row of holes into it at the same interval as the grippers. Fasten the base along the floor so the holes line up with the clamps.

SHOP TIP

Storing handscrews

For small clamps like handscrews, it is often unnecessary to build separate storage. An exposed stud can serve as an effective clamping post. Avoid storing clamps directly overhead, should vibration cause one to fall. If your shop has a finished ceiling and walls, install a length of 2-by-4 across the legs of your bench and secure your clamps to the stock.

STORING SMALL ITEMS

Mounting glass jars under a shelf
Screws, nails, and bolts can be stored in a variety of containers, including tennis ball canisters, mason jars, or pill bottles. Mounting the containers under a shelf *(above)* will keep the items out in the open without cluttering a work surface. Fasten the container lid to the shelf, then screw the container to the lid.

SHOP TIP

Storing sanding disks
Leaving sanding disks loose in a drawer or on a workbench risks damaging them. To sort disks, use a storage box for 5¼-inch computer diskettes. These boxes come with partitions that can be labeled to separate disks of different grits.

BUILD IT YOURSELF

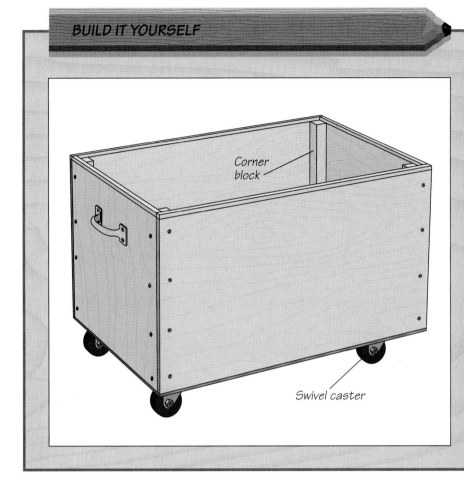

A SCRAPBOX

Use a scrapbox to keep from cluttering the shop floor with cut-offs, shavings, and other refuse. The design shown at left can be built quickly from ¾-inch plywood; casters allow the unit to be rolled where it is needed and moved out of the way when it is not. Saw the sides and bottom to a size appropriate to your needs, then cut four corner blocks from 2-by-2 stock. Screw the four sides together, driving the screws into the corner blocks. Turn the box over and nail the bottom to the corner blocks and sides. Add a lip around the top to hide the plywood edges. Finally, screw casters to each bottom corner and a pull handle at one end.

Some storage devices, particularly those designed for small items, are less trouble to buy than to build. The system shown at left features open plastic bins that can be lined up or stacked. The bins are suspended from plastic strips that are screwed to the wall.

WORK SURFACES

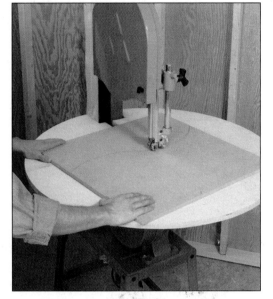

Better control produces better results. Secured to a band saw's original table, a shop-made extension table keeps a large hardboard sheet level during a curved cut.

It is a truism that no workshop is ever large enough; it is equally true that no woodworker ever has enough tables, benches, sawhorses, stands, or props to support work in progress. The traditional workbench, however useful or necessary *(see page 46)*, is only the beginning. For many uses, it is too high, too small, or too immobile to be helpful.

When it is time to mark the elements of a joint or assemble the many pieces of a chair, a solid work table, like the library-style table shown on page 113, can serve as the command center of your shop, becoming the focus of many operations. This design features a spacious work surface and sturdy construction. The only drawback is size: one would need a fairly large shop to accommodate this table. For a smaller shop with cramped quarters, consider the folding table featured on page 115. Offering almost as much surface area as the library-style version, it can be folded out of the way against the wall when it is not needed. The temporary table illustrated on page 117 offers yet another solution to the constant conflict between space and convenience, satisfying both the need for a substantial working surface and ease of storage. Resting on sawhorses, this plywood sheet tabletop can be set up whenever a flat surface is required, then be dismantled and put away when your project moves on to another phase.

With its myriad uses, the sawhorse is also the workhorse of the shop. A sawhorse can serve as a set of legs for a fold-down work table *(page 116)* or a simple prop for sawing stock. With a few notches cut into their crosspieces, horses can form part of the frame for a shop-made glue rack *(page 124)*. Clamped to a 2-by-4 attached to a commercial roller, a sawhorse becomes a custom-built roller stand.

Outfeed tables and roller stands that hold unwieldy panels or long planks significantly expand the versatility of tools like table saws, band saws, and drill presses. Set up at the same level as a machine's table, or fractionally below it, these props can be as welcome as a second set of hands, enhancing a tool's capacity to handle large workpieces efficiently and safely.

Work surfaces can even be rigged to compensate for a lack of full-size stationary machines. The stand shown on page 134 is designed to let you mount a benchtop tool at a comfortable working height. The three-in-one tool table featured on page 136 can transform a router, saber saw, and electric drill into mini-stationary tools.

Given a need and a few pieces of wood, every woodworker will devise some way to improve his or her tools. The examples that follow are mere suggestions, for it is impossible to limit the imagination when the need arises for improving the workshop.

The door of this storage cabinet folds down from a shop wall to become a sturdy work surface. Supported by solid lumber legs, it is an ideal work table for light-duty operations such as gluing up and assembling small carcases. For details on how to built this unit, see page 98.

WORK TABLES

Almost as strong as a traditional workbench, this commercial work table is a versatile workhorse, especially when paired with a woodworker's vise. The cabinet and drawers provide storage space, and can be locked to secure valuable tools.

For many light woodworking chores, from marking out joints to assembling pieces of furniture, a simple work table fits the bill as well as a traditional woodworker's bench. This section features several table designs. All are quick, easy, and inexpensive to build. The table shown opposite is sufficiently large and sturdy for most jobs; if space is at a premium, a good compromise would be one of the fold-up versions shown on pages 115 and 116. You can also conserve space by incorporating storage shelves, drawers, or cabinets in your design. For assembling carcases and other pieces of furniture, you may find the low-to-the-ground table on page 114 handier than a standard-height work surface.

Whichever design you choose, be careful of the nails or screws you use to construct a table—particularly when fastening the tabletop to the frame. Take the time to countersink or counterbore screw heads and set nail heads below the surface to prevent the fasteners from marring your work.

Despite its lightweight, compact design, the Black & Decker Workmate™ can support loads up to 550 pounds. It also folds virtually flat for easy storage. A special pivot design allows the vise jaws to be angled, for securing workpieces like the tapered leg shown in the photo. This particular Workmate™ features a storage tray and a top that flips up for vertical clamping. The Workmate™ has a long, colorful history. By 1968, the prototype, featuring a patented folding H-frame, had been rejected by every major tool manufacturer in Britain. Four years later, the inventor of the Workmate™, Ron Hickman, persuaded Black & Decker in England to mass produce his invention. International distribution rights were negotiated the following year. Popular success for the Workmate™ was almost immediate: Worldwide sales of the table are close to 20 million units—and counting.

A LIBRARY-TYPE WORK TABLE

The all-purpose table shown below is built with a combination of lumber and plywood. Refer to the dimensions in the illustration for a work surface that is 5 feet long, 3 feet wide, and 3 feet high.

Saw the legs to length from 4-by-4 stock, then prepare them for the rails: Cut a two-shouldered tenon at the top end of each leg with shoulders ¾ inch wide *(inset)*. Next, cut the rails, stretchers, and braces to length from 2-by-4s. Saw miters at both ends of the braces so that one end sits flush against the inside edge of the legs and the other end butts against the bottom of the rails. Prepare the front, back, and side rails for assembly by beveling their ends and cutting rabbets to accommodate the leg tenons *(inset)*. Screw the stretchers to the rails, spread glue on the contacting surfaces of the legs and rails, fit the pieces together, and screw the rails to the legs. Next, attach the braces to the legs and rails with screws.

Cut the tabletop from ¾-inch plywood and screw it to the rails. Finally, cut a piece of ¼-inch hardboard to the same dimensions as the top and nail it to the plywood as a replaceable protective cover. Be sure to set the nail heads below the surface.

Stretcher rails
1 ½" x 3 ½" x 33"

Tabletop
¾" x 36" x 60"

Brace
1 ½" x 3 ½" x 12"

Front rail
1 ½" x 3 ½" x 60"

Side rail
1 ½" x 3 ½" x 36"

Leg
3 ½" x 3 ½" x 36"

Rail

Leg

Front and back rails
1 1/2" x 3 1/2" x 29"

Side rails
1 1/2" x 3 1/2" x 19"

Braces
1 1/2" x 3 1/2" x 16"

Legs
3 1/2" x 3 1/2" x 25"

Cover
1/4" x 28" x 35"

Tabletop
3/4" x 28" x 35"

Building a low assembly table

For operations that are awkward to perform on a standard-height table, use an assembly table like the one shown at left. Ideal for jobs like gluing up carcases, the table can be built easily in the shop with a small amount of wood. Refer to the dimensions in the illustration for a work surface that is about 12 inches lower than a standard table. Saw the legs from 4-by-4 stock and the rails and braces from 2-by-4s; cut miters at the ends of the braces so they butt against the legs and sit flush with the top of the rails. Screw the rails to the legs, then fasten the braces to the legs and rails *(inset)*. Next, saw the tabletop from 3/4-inch plywood; it will overhang the rails by about 3 inches on all sides. Screw the top to the rails, countersinking the fasteners. Cut a replaceable cover from 1/4-inch hardboard and nail it to the tabletop; set the nail heads below the surface of the cover.

STOW-AWAY WORK TABLES

Hinge

Top
3/4" x 20" x 48"

Leg
1 1/2" x 3 1/2" x 35"

Brace
1 1/2" x 3 1/2" x 14 1/2 "

Front rail
1 1/2" x 3 1/2" x 45"

Shim
3/4" x 1 1/2" x 4"

Side rail
1 1/2" x 3 1/2" x 18 1/2"

Making and installing a fold-down work table

The table shown above incorporates a large and sturdy work surface, but still conserves space by folding up against a wall when it is not in use. The dimensions in the illustration yield a work surface measuring 20 by 48 inches. Cut the bracing, legs, rails, and stretchers from 2-by-4 stock and screw the bracing between the wall studs *(inset)*; there should be one brace for every pair of studs along the table's length. Fasten the front legs to the side rails using carriage bolts and lock nuts; place washers on both sides of the legs. Leave the bolts just loose enough to allow the legs to pivot when the table is folded up. To complete the frame,

attach the front rails to the side rails. Add a 45-inch-long top rear rail and fasten two 17-inch-long stretchers between the rear rail and the top front rail to provide added support for the top. Next, screw the top to the rails, countersinking the fasteners. To allow the table to fold down without binding, screw shims to the ends of the bottom side rails, then attach the table to the bracing with butt hinges; use two hinges for each outside brace. Finally, drive an eye bolt into the bottom front rail and a catch into the wall to secure the table when it is folded up.

Notched
2-by-4

Work surface

Supporting a fold-down work surface on sawhorses
Rather than building a framework for a fold-down work surface, you can use a panel of ¾-inch plywood hinged to the
wall and supported by sawhorses. The surface can be of any
size. Begin by setting the panel on two sawhorses; one edge
of the panel should be flush against the wall. Mark a point
on the panel at every wall stud, then install butt hinges,
screwing one leaf of each hinge to a stud and the other leaf
to the panel at a pencil mark. To secure the panel when it is
folded up, screw a notched piece of 2-by-4 to the stud closest to the middle of the panel at a height that will allow the
notched end to slip over the edge of the panel *(inset)*.

Tabletop support

³/₄" plywood

Crosspiece

Notches

SHOP TIP

Stabilizing a temporary work surface

Tables consisting of ply-wood panels laid across two sawhorses are a cinch to set up, but they tend to slide and twist. Attaching cleats to the underside of the panel on either side of the sawhorses' crosspieces helps to stabilize these makeshift work surfaces. To position the cleats, mark the outline of each crosspiece on the panel, then screw a length of 1-by-3 to the panel on either side of each out-line, leaving as little clearance as possible between the cleats and the crosspieces. For extra stability, attach 1-by-3s between the pairs of cleats to serve as rails.

Setting up a temporary work surface

Consisting of two sawhorses, six 2-by-4s and a plywood panel, the unit shown above is inexpensive and easy to put together, yet it provides a large and sta-ble work surface that can be set up and disassembled quickly. Start by fitting the sawhorses with crosspieces cut from 2-by-6 stock, then cut the 2-by-4s to the same length as the panel. In three of the boards, cut a notch about 8 inch-es from each end; the notches should be about 2 inches deep and as wide as the thickness of the crosspieces. Cut matching notches in the top edges of the crosspieces. Center the unnotched edge of the notched boards along the face of the other 2-by-4s and screw them together to form three T-shaped tabletop supports. The sawhorse sup-ports can be used to hold a large sheet of plywood for ripping, or a permanent top can be screwed to the 2-by-4s.

SAWHORSES

S awhorses have countless uses in the woodworking shop, from table legs to tool stands. Occasionally it seems that their original purpose—to support boards for sawing—is only an afterthought. It is easy to see why sawhorses are considered so versatile, for their compact design makes them especially useful in shops with limited floor space. Some commercial models, like the ones in the photo at right, can be adjusted to different heights and folded up for easy storage. With commercial brackets *(below)*, you can size sawhorses to suit your needs. The shop-made horses featured on page 119 can be disassembled and put away after use.

Different operations require different-sized sawhorses. For supporting stock for handsawing or holding large workpieces at a comfortable height, small horses about 18 inches high are ideal. Taller sawhorses are needed if they are to be used to hold up a work surface

or as outfeed supports for a table saw. They should be about ¼ inch lower than the saw table. Whatever the dimensions of your sawhorses, never make them taller than their length, as they will tend to be unstable.

This sawhorse features leg extensions that can be adjusted to a variety of heights. The legs retract into the crosspiece, making the unit compact and portable. A pair of these slender metal horses can support one ton of material.

MAKING SAWHORSES

Using commercial sawhorse brackets

A pair of metal sawhorse brackets can help you transform a couple of 2-by-4s and 1-by-3s into a sturdy sawhorse, like the one shown at right. Saw the legs and crosspiece from 2-by-4s, then cut a bevel at the bottom of the legs so they will sit flat on the floor. Fit the legs into the bottom of the brackets, insert the crosspiece and spread the legs; the brackets will grip the crosspiece and stabilize the horse. Screw the brackets to the legs and crosspiece. For added stability, add braces and a stretcher. The braces are cut from 1-by-3s and screwed to the legs, making sure that the ends are flush with the outside faces of the legs. For the stretcher, cut a 1-by-3 to size and screw it between the braces.

Metal bracket

Crosspiece

Leg

Stretcher

Brace

Crosspiece

Cleat

Leg

SHOP TIP

Stacking sawhorses

If you want to stack your sawhorses, instead of the type of braces seen on page 118, make plywood braces like those shown at right. Cut a notch in each brace so it will mesh with the crosspiece of the sawhorse beneath it. To prevent the stack from toppling over, be sure the fit is snug by leaving only a small amount of clearance in the notches.

Building a knock-down sawhorse

With only a small amount of lumber and plywood and a few minutes' time, you can make a sturdy, knock-down sawhorse like the one shown above. Cut the legs from ¾-inch plywood, then saw a 3-inch-deep notch in the middle of the top of both pieces. Next, cut the crosspiece from 1-by-6 stock and saw a 1½-inch-deep slot 8 inches in from either end to fit into the legs. Angle the slots roughly 5° from the vertical so the legs spread slightly outward. For added stability, screw 4-inch-long 1-by-2 cleats to the crosspiece on each side of the slots.

Leg

Crosspiece

Stretcher

Foot

WEDGED MORTISE-AND-TENON JOINT

Assembling a frame-and-foot sawhorse
Lightweight, compact frame-and-foot sawhorses like the one shown at left can be built from 2-by-4 stock. Start by cutting the legs to a suitable height, then prepare them to join to the other parts of the unit: Cut tenons at the bottom ends, rout through mortises halfway up the faces, and saw 1-inch-deep notches in the middle of the top ends. Cut the feet to length and, for added stability, cut recesses along their bottom edges, leaving a 2-inch pad at each end. Rout mortises through the middle of the feet for the leg tenons. Next, saw the stretcher to fit between the legs and cut tenons at both ends. Cut the crosspiece and saw a notch 4 inches from either end that will fit into the notch at the top of the legs. To reinforce the mortise-and-tenon joints, saw a pair of kerfs in the end of each tenon and make wedges to fit into the kerfs *(inset)*. Tap the wedges in to expand the tenon when the joint is assembled.

SHOP TIP

Padding sawhorses
To prevent a sawhorse from marring your work, cover its crosspiece with a strip of old carpet. Fold the carpet over the top edge of the crosspiece and screw it to the sides. For a smoother surface, use an old towel or blanket rather than a piece of carpet.

Crosspiece

Stretcher

Brace

Leg

Making a heavy-duty sawhorse

Reinforced by a stretcher, braces, and simple joinery, the sawhorse shown above will endure for years as a sturdy work surface. Saw the crosspiece to length from a 2-by-6 and cut dadoes in the edges about 4 inches from either end to accommodate the legs. Angle the dadoes roughly 10° from the vertical. Next, saw the 2-by-4 legs to length and cut 1½-inch-deep angled notches into their outside edges to house the braces. The top of each brace should rest about 1½ inches below the tops of the legs. Also cut bevels at both ends of the legs so they will sit flat on the floor and lie flush with the crosspiece. The stretcher is a 2-by-4 cut to the same length as the crosspiece; cut a notch in each end to line up with the brace, leaving a 1½-inch shoulder. Saw the braces from 2-by-6 stock, mitering the ends to be flush with the outside faces of the legs and sawing a 2-inch deep notch in the middle of the top edge for the stretcher. Finally, glue up the sawhorse, strengthening the joints between the legs, crosspieces, and braces with screws.

Corner half-lap joint

T half-lap joint

Piano hinge

Top rails
¾" x 5½" x 36"

Hinged crossbrace
¾" x 5½" x 16"

Bottom rails
¾" x 5½" x 36"

Legs
¾" x 5½" x 34"

Building a folding sawhorse

Made entirely from 1-by-6 stock, with a hinged crossbrace and top, this lightweight sawhorse folds flat to store easily in even the most cramped workshop. Cut the legs and rails to length. Then, cut notches in the pieces for half-lap joints. Use T-type half-laps *(inset, bottom)* to join the legs to the bottom rails, and corner half-laps *(inset, top)* to join the top rails to the legs. Assemble and glue the two sections of the horse, and reinforce the joints with screws. When the glue has cured, join the two sections at the top rails with a continuous piano hinge. Finally, cut the crossbrace; be sure it is long enough so when the horse legs spread, the piano hinge is recessed between the top rails. Saw the crossbrace in half and connect the pieces with a piano hinge, making sure that the hinge is installed so the brace will pivot upwards. Then, fasten the crossbrace to both side rails, again using piano hinges.

SHOP TIP

Securing workpieces edge-up on sawhorses
Clamp handscrews to the crosspieces of two sawhorses to support work edge-up when a bench vise is not available. To prevent the handscrews from pivoting, secure each with two C clamps as shown. Use as many sawhorses and handscrews as needed to adequately support the piece.

Notched wood block
1½" x 3½" x 4"

Sawhorse panel support frame

When sawing large panels, proper support is needed to keep the work from buckling and binding on the blade as the cut is made, and to stop the cutoff from falling away as the cut is finished. To accommodate these cumbersome jobs, construct this 4-by-8-foot support frame, which is easily held in place with notched wood blocks. Cut two 4-foot and two 8-foot lengths of 2-by-4 for the ends and sides of the frame. Cut dadoes six inches from the ends of the 4-foot lengths and 18 inches from the ends of the 8-foot lengths for the cross half-lap joints that hold the frame together as shown. Then cut two 4-inch-long blocks from 2-by-4 and saw a two-inch-deep notch, wide enough to fit over 1½-by-1½-inch deep notches in the middle of the crosspieces of the sawhorses you plan to use. Screw the blocks to the bottom of the end pieces and assemble and glue up the frame. Secure the frame to the sawhorses by mating the notches in the blocks with those in the crosspieces.

A VARIABLE-HEIGHT WORK SURFACE

Corner lap joint

¾" x 3½" x 29"

¾" x 3½" x 30"

¾" x 3½" x 22¼"

¾" x 3½" x 23¼"

Building the box

Constructing a box with different width, length, and height dimensions will provide you with a work surface that can be used at three levels. The top surface of the box shown at right, for example, can be either 24, 30, or 36 inches high. Saw all the pieces from 1-by-4 stock, making four boards 30 inches long, eight 29 inches long, another four 22¼ inches long and eight more 23¼ inches long. Use a lightweight wood like pine to make the box easily portable. Assemble the box in two steps, gluing up the six sides individually, then joining them together. To make each side, cut rabbets at both ends of each board and glue up the boards with a lap joint *(inset)*. Once the glue has cured, cut a rabbet along the outside edges of all the sides, and glue up the sides into a carcase. If you choose to reinforce the joinery at the corners with screws, be sure to countersink the screw heads.

SHOP TIP

A shop-made glue rack

A rack made from two metal-bracket type sawhorses provides a convenient way to hold bar clamps for gluing up panels. To build the jig, replace the crosspiece of your sawhorses with substitutes that are at least as long as the boards to be glued together. Notch one edge of each crosspiece at 6-inch intervals, making the cuts wide enough to hold a bar clamp snugly and deep enough to hold the bar level with the top of the crosspiece.

WORK SUPPORTS

Supporting long planks and large panels as they are fed across a saw table ranks as one of the most cumbersome tasks in the woodworking shop. Outfeed tables can be attached to most saws, but they tend to take up a lot of floor space. Once side supports are added to your machine, your shop may become an obstacle course.

Commercial roller stands, like the one shown in the photo at right, make better use of shop space; they can also be moved easily to where they are needed and adjusted to whatever height is suitable. The shop-made stands described below and on the following page share the advantages of the store-bought variety, with the additional benefit of being easy and inexpensive to build. They can also be dismantled and stored when not needed.

There are other work-support jigs that make life easier in the shop. The vise extension stand shown on page 127, for example, solves the problem of keeping long boards edge-up in a bench vise.

A commercial roller stand supports a board being ripped on a radial arm saw. The stand should typically be set ¼-inch below the level of the saw table and positioned two feet from its edge.

TWO SHOP-MADE ROLLER STANDS

Roller

Mast

Guide

Brace

Setting up a temporary stand

With only a sawhorse, two C clamps, and a commercial roller, you can make a simple roller stand like the one shown at left. Make a T-shaped mast for the roller that is long enough to hold it at a suitable height. Screw the roller to the horizontal part of the mast. Add a brace to the side of the horse for clamping the mast in place: Cut a 1-by-4 to span the legs between the sawhorse bracket and the original brace and screw it to the legs. Cut a 1-by-2 to span the two braces and screw it in place as a vertical guide for the mast. To secure the roller stand to the sawhorse, clamp the mast to the braces, making sure it is flush against the guide.

Building an adjustable roller stand

To build the roller stand shown at right, start by constructing the frame for the roller, cutting the four pieces from 1-by-4 stock. Glue the frame together with butt joints, adding screws to reinforce the connections. Then bore a hole in the middle of each side of the frame for a ¼-inch-diameter carriage bolt. Locate the hole 3 inches from the bottom of the frame. Insert the bolts from the inside of the frame and screw the roller to the top. As well as the commercial roller shown, two variations that permit you to feed the workpiece from any direction are shown below. Cut the remaining pieces of the stand from 1-by-6 stock, referring to the dimensions provided, then rout a ¼-inch-wide slot down the middle of the two uprights; the slot should be about 14 inches long. Screw the crosspiece to the uprights, aligning the top of the piece with the bottom of the slot. Fasten the uprights and rails to the feet. To guide the roller frame, nail 1-by-1 cleats to the uprights about ¼ inch in from the edges. To set up the stand, position the roller frame between the uprights, fitting the carriage bolts into the slots. Slip washers on the bolts and tighten the wing nuts to set the height of the roller.

Frame
3 ½" x 10" x 18"

Roller

Carriage bolt

Cleat
³/₄" x ³/₄" x 14"

Crosspiece
³/₄" x 5 ½" x 18"

Slot

Foot
³/₄" x 5 ½" x 18"

Upright
³/₄" x 5 ½" x 30"

Rail
³/₄" x 5 ½" x 20"

TYPES OF ROLLERS

Plate-mounted casters

Commercial roller balls

A VISE EXTENSION STAND

Support piece

Swivel bar
$\frac{1}{2}$" x 1" x 4 $\frac{1}{2}$"

Support piece
1 $\frac{1}{4}$" x 1 $\frac{5}{8}$" x 7"

Dowel
$\frac{3}{8}$" x 2 $\frac{1}{2}$"

Notch

Upright
$\frac{3}{4}$" x 1 $\frac{1}{2}$" x 30"

Foot
1 $\frac{1}{2}$" x 2 $\frac{1}{4}$" x 13"

Making and using the stand

Also known as a bench slave, a vise extension stand is used to support the free end of a long board clamped in the shoulder vise of a workbench. Refer to the dimensions in the illustration for a stand that works well with most workbenches.

To build the stand, cut the upright to length and, starting 5 inches from the bottom, saw angled notches at 2½-inch intervals along its length. Cut the notches about 1 inch long and ½ inch wide. Then saw the feet to length and cut recesses along their bottom edges. Join the feet with a cross lap joint: Cut a lap in the top edge of one foot and in the bottom edge of the

other foot. Glue the two feet together. Once the adhesive is dry, screw the upright to the feet. Cut the support piece and swivel bars, angling the top of the support piece about 10° *(inset)*. To join the support piece to the swivel bars, bore holes for ⅜-inch-diameter dowels through the piece and near the ends of the bars, and slip the dowels into the holes; glue them in place. To use the stand, insert the dowel at the top end of the swivel bars in the appropriate slot in the upright for the height you need and prop your workpiece on the support piece.

CUTTING LARGE PANELS ON THE BAND SAW

Pivot point
Support bracket
Foot

Making and using the jig

For making circular cuts out of large panels on the band saw, use a jig like the one shown above. Build the jig from ¾-inch plywood, cutting the pieces so the top of the jig is level with the saw table when the feet are screwed or clamped to a work table. Before assembling the jig, drive a 1¼-inch-long screw as a pivot point through the center of the top piece so the tip of the screw projects from the surface by about ½ inch *(inset)*. Then screw the top and feet to the sides of the jig, and attach the triangular-shaped support brackets to the top and sides; be sure to counter-sink the fasteners. Before setting up the jig, mark the center and circumference of the circle on the workpiece. Then cut from the edge of the piece to the marked circumference and back to the edge, creating a starting point for the circular cut. Now set up the jig: Attach it to a table and place the workpiece on the jig so the marked center of the circle contacts the pivot point. Position the table so the blade butts against the marked circle and the pivot point is aligned with the center of the blade and the machine's center line. Cut the circle by rotating the workpiece into the blade.

EXTENSION TABLES

Stationary machines like table saws, band saws, and drill presses come from the manufacturer equipped with tables that are adequate for most routine operations. But there are some tasks—crosscutting long planks or panels on the table saw, performing long cuts on the band saw, and smoothing large pieces with a sanding drum on the drill press—that can be awkward or even dangerous to attempt without extending the size of the machine's table. Often, the solution creates a new problem, however, because increasing the size of a stationary machine with a permanent addition can crowd even the roomiest workshop.

The following pages illustrate a variety of devices for extending the work area of woodworking machines. Although easy to build and use, each jig is designed to be removed or folded out of the way.

An extension table greatly simplifies the task of crosscutting wide panels on the table saw. This commercial model more than doubles the saw table's surface area. It also features a specially designed rip fence that can be moved to any position across the table.

SHOP TIP

Double-duty work table
To get maximum use from the work table in your shop, build it so the top is at the same height or slightly lower than the level of your table saw. In addition to being a handy work surface for light jobs, the table can butt against the saw table to serve as an outfeed support. If necessary, modify the table to mate tightly with your saw by cutting a notch in the top to clear the blade guard or other obstructions.

EXTENSION TABLES

Building an extension table for a radial arm saw

Made entirely from 2-by-4 and 1-by-3 stock, the extension table shown above can be attached to the outfeed or infeed ends of a radial arm saw table. Using 2-by-4s, cut the legs, rails, and stretchers to suit the dimensions of your saw, making the length of the legs equal to the distance between the top of the saw table and the shop floor, less the thickness of the stretchers. Attach the rail stretchers so that their tops are flush with the rail's top edges. Attach the leg stretchers to the legs, then screw the legs to the inside edges of the rails. Make certain the outside rail stretcher is butted against the tops of the legs. Cut the braces from 1-by-3s to reach from the bottom of the second rail stretcher to the inside edges of

the legs. Miter the ends of the braces and screw them in place. To fasten the extension table to the saw table shown, cut two wood strips and screw one end of each piece to the underside of the inside rail stretcher. Set the extension table flush against the saw table and fasten the other end of the strips to the underside of the table, using shims or spacers as needed. If you prefer to span the table's rails with rollers *(inset)*, rather than wood stretchers, cut the rail stretchers long enough to fasten them to the bottom edge of the rails. Then screw commercial rollers to the tops of the stretchers, placing shims under the rollers, if necessary, to set them level with the top of the saw table.

Outfitting a table saw with a fold-down outfeed table

A handy extension to your saw table for cutting long stock, the shop-made jig shown above swings down out of the way when it is not needed. Start by cutting the top, sides, and support brackets from ¾-inch plywood, sizing the pieces to suit your needs. Then saw the braces and cleat from 1-by-2 stock, adding an angled notch at the bottom end of both braces. Screw the sides to the top, countersinking the fasteners. Next, get ready to attach the jig to the saw housing. First, attach an angle iron to each side of both support brackets. Then, have a helper hold the top against the saw table, making sure the two surfaces are level; leave a slight gap between the top and saw table so the jig will fold down without jamming against the table. Now determine the position of the support brackets by butting each against the inside face of a side piece. Mark the holes in the angle irons on the saw housing. Drill a hole for a machine screw at each mark and fasten the angle irons to the housing. Reposition the jig against the saw table and bore holes for a carriage bolt through the sides and support brackets. Use washers under the nuts and bolt heads, and between the sides and brackets. Attach the braces to the sides with bolts spaced about 8 inches from the bracket bolts. Leave all the bolts loose enough for the sides and braces to pivot. Then, holding the jig level again, swing the braces toward the saw housing. Mark the points where the braces contact the housing and screw a cleat to the housing so the cleat's top surface aligns with the two points. To set the jig in position, rest the braces on the cleat. To fold the table down *(inset)*, raise the top slightly, move the braces off the cleat and swing the jig down.

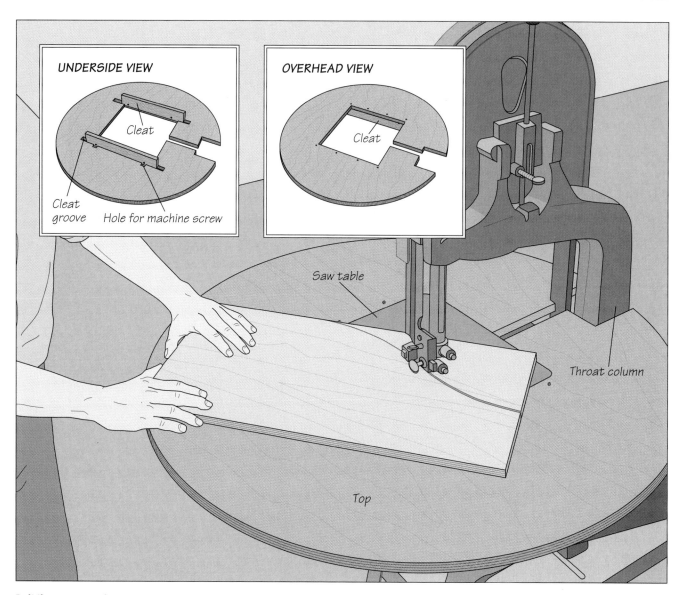

Building an extension table for a band saw

An auxiliary band saw table will significantly increase the machine's versatility. The extension table shown above is especially handy for cutting long or wide pieces. Using ¾-inch plywood, cut the top of the jig to a suitable diameter. Cut out the center and the edge to fit the top around the saw table and throat column. Saw a 1½-inch-wide channel between the cutouts so the top can be installed without removing the blade. Next, prepare two cleats that will be used to attach the saw table to the jig top. For these, two 1-by-3s should be cut a few inches longer than the saw table. Then position each one in turn against the side of the saw table with threaded holes, so that they are ¾ inch below the table surface, with at least ¼ inch of stock above the holes. (Make sure your machine has these holes; most band saws have them for mounting an accessory rip fence.) Depending on the position of the threaded holes on your saw table, you may have to position the top of the cleats closer than ¾ inch to the machine tabletop. In that case you will have to rout grooves for the cleats on the underside of the top to allow the tabletop to sit flush with the machine's table *(inset, left)*. Mark the hole locations on the cleats, bore a hole at each spot, and fasten the cleats to the saw table with the screws provided for the rip fence. Then place the tabletop on the cleats and screw it in place *(inset, right)*; be sure to countersink the screws. The top should sit level with the saw table. You may need to cut clearance notches so that you can reach the machine screws once the jig is completed. To remove the jig, loosen only the machine screws, leaving the cleats attached to the top permanently.

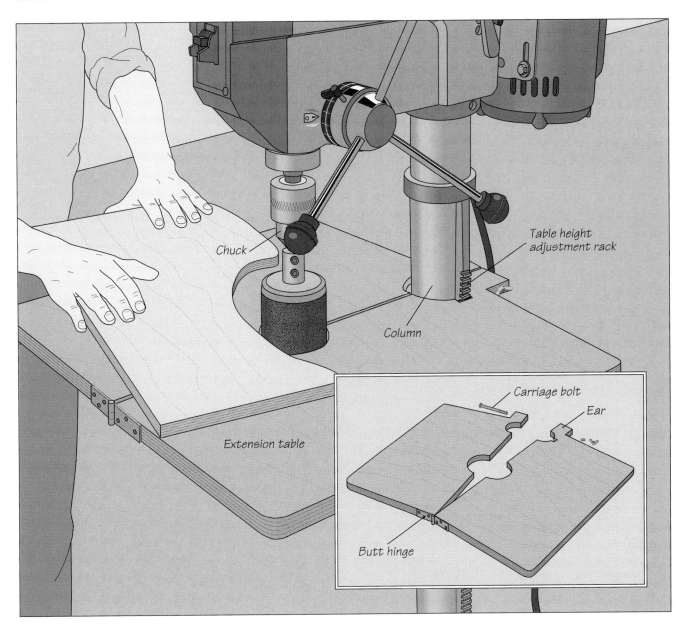

Chuck

Table height
adjustment rack

Column

Extension table

Carriage bolt

Ear

Butt hinge

Fitting a drill press with an extension table

The small table typical of most drill presses will not adequately support many large workpieces. A customized extension table for the tool will enable you to keep a workpiece level as you feed it into an accessory like a sanding drum *(above)*. Start by cutting a piece of ¾-inch plywood into a square with dimensions that suit your needs. Then mark a line down the middle of the piece and draw two circles centered on the line. Locate one about 4 inches from the back edge, sizing it to fit snugly around the drill press column. Locate the second hole under the chuck; make its diameter about ½ inch greater than the largest accessory you plan to insert into the chuck. To help you pinpoint the center of hole,

install a bit in the chuck and measure the distance from the column to the bit. Prepare to install the jig on the drill press table by cutting two recesses along its back edge, leaving a rectangular "ear" that protrudes behind the back hole. Then bore a hole through the ear for a ¼-inch-diameter carriage bolt. Next, saw the jig in two along the centerline and cut out the two circles. You may need to make other cuts to clear protrusions on your particular drill press. On the model shown, a notch was needed for the table height adjustment rack. Finally, screw a butt hinge to the front edge of the jig to join the two halves together *(inset)*. The carriage bolt and wing nut will clamp the table in place.

TOOL STANDS AND TABLES

A stand or table can transform a portable power tool into a reasonable facsimile of a full-size stationary machine. What they concede in power to their larger cousins, bench-mounted tools compensate with portability, ease of storage, and lower price.

There are commercial stands for benchtop tools, but you can easily build a stand like the one shown below. Storage shelves and drawers can be added to customize the basic design. There is one requirement, however: Ensure the stand's surface area is large enough for your needs and that it supports the tool at a comfortable height. The extension router table shown opposite not only converts a router into a mini-shaper, but can be easily removed when it is not needed. A more elaborate, but versatile option is illustrated on page 136. The three-in-one portable power tool table features replaceable inserts for a router, an electric drill, and a saber saw.

Because of its central role in woodworking, the router merits a dedicated table in most shops. The shop-built benchtop version illustrated on page 139 allows you to take advantage of this tool's great versatility.

Held upside down in a commercial table, a router becomes a stationary tool. Here, it is cutting a groove for a sliding dovetail joint. Many woodworkers consider the router table to be the single most important accessory you can add to your tool.

SUPPORTS FOR PORTABLE POWER TOOLS

Building a benchtop tool stand

The stand shown at right is constructed from 4-by-4 and 2-by-4 lumber and plywood. Saw the legs from 4-by-4s and the rails from 2-by-4s, sizing the pieces to suit your needs. Notch the legs at the top and 6 inches down from the top to fit the rails, then cut matching rabbets at the ends of all the rails *(inset)*. Glue up the legs and rails, adding countersunk screws to reinforce the joints. Cut the top from ¾-inch plywood. If you plan to place a table saw on the stand, saw a square hole out of the center of the top as shown to allow sawdust to fall through; place a box underneath to catch the waste. Finally, screw the top to the legs and rails, again countersinking the fasteners. When using a tool on the stand, secure it to the top with screws or clamps.

134

Making and mounting a removable router table

Attached to a workbench or table, the extension table shown above serves as a compact router table that can be stored when it is not needed. Size the parts according to your needs. Start by cutting the top from ³⁄₄-inch plywood, and the rails and braces from 2-by-4 stock. Saw the rails 6 inches longer than the width of the top so they extend under the top and can be fastened to the underside of the bench using nuts and hanger bolts. The hinged braces should be long enough to reach from the underside of the rails to a leg rail on the bench. Cut a bevel at the top end of the braces and an angled notch at the bottom end. The router is attached to the top with a square sub-base made of ¹⁄₄-inch clear acrylic. Several steps are necessary to fit the base to the tabletop and then to the router. First, lay the square sub-base in the center of the table, clamp it in place, and mark its edges with a pencil. Mark the center of the sub-base and drill a pilot hole completely through the base and the tabletop. Remove the sub-base and turn your attention to the tabletop. Use your router to plow a ¹⁄₄-inch-deep recess within the pencil outline of the sub-base. Then, using the pilot hole as a center and your router as a template, cut a round hole through the tabletop the size of your router's standard base. The tabletop is now ready. In the sub-base, drill a hole in the center that is slightly larger than your largest router bit, and screw the base to the router, using countersunk machine screws. Lay the sub-base in the table recess and screw it down, countersinking the wood screws. All surfaces should be flush. For a fence, cut two pieces of ³⁄₄-inch plywood and screw them together in an L shape. Saw a notch out of the fence's bottom edge to accommodate your largest bit, then screw on four fence supports for added stability. Attach a clear semicircular plastic guard with a hinge to allow it to be raised out of the way (inset). The fence is clamped in place.

PORTABLE POWER TOOL TABLE

Easy and inexpensive to build, the versatile table shown below allows you to convert three different portable power tools into stationary tools: the electric drill, the router, and the saber saw. The table features a spacious tabletop, an adjustable fence, a storage shelf, and a conveniently located On/off switch. The tabletop includes a rectangular cutout to accept a custom-made insert for each of the three power tools.

Use ¾-inch plywood for the tabletop, the shelf, the cleats, the inserts

Guard
Fence
Support bracket
Insert
Miter gauge slot
On/off switch
Top rail
Shelf
Bottom rail
Leg

CUTTING LIST
— **Tabletop:** ¾" x 25" x 40"
— **Legs (4):** 1½" x 3½" x 30"
— **Support brackets (6):** ¼" x 9" x 9"
— **Front and back rails (4):** ¾" x 2½" x 40"
— **Side rails (4):** ¾" x 2½" x 25"
— **Shelf:** ¾" x 25" x 33"
— **Cleats (2):** ¾" x 3" x 9½"
— **Cleats (2):** ¾" x 5" x 16"
— **Inserts (3):** ¾" x 12½" x 14½"

and the fence; $1/4$-inch plywood for the support brackets; and solid lumber for the other parts (2-by-4s for the legs and 1-by-3s for the rails). Refer to the cutting list for suggested dimensions.

Start building the table by preparing the tabletop for the tool inserts. Cut a rectangular hole out of its center the same size as the inserts. Then screw the cleats to the underside of the top, forming a ledge to which the inserts can be fastened (below). Before assembling the table, rout a $3/8$-inch-deep dado across the table about 12 inches from the left-hand end to accommodate a miter gauge. Then screw the parts of the table together. Use lap joints for the top rails (placed flat), then screw this frame onto the top of the legs. Screw the bottom rails (placed on edge) to the legs, then attach the shelf. You can either countersink the fasteners or counterbore the holes, and then conceal the screw heads with wood plugs.

Next, saw the three tool inserts, sizing them to fit precisely in the hole in the tabletop. Prepare the router insert as you would the top of the removable

Router base plate

Router insert

Acrylic sub-base

Cleat

router table shown on page 135. To mount the insert in the table, set it in place on the cleats and bore a hole through the insert and the cleats at each corner; the holes should be countersunk. Screw the insert to the cleats.

For the electric drill insert, bore a hole through the center of the insert that is slightly wider than the largest accessory you plan to use. Then screw a commercial drill guide to the underside of the insert so the drill chuck will be centered in the hole. (You may need to drill holes through the base of the drill guide to fasten it in place.) The bit or accessory in the drill chuck should protrude from the top of the insert without the chuck being visible. Place wooden washers under the guide rods of the drill guide to

UNDERSIDE VIEW

Drill guide

Washer

Electric drill insert

UNDERSIDE VIEW

Saber saw insert

adjust the height of the drill, if necessary *(above)*.

For the saber saw insert, position the tool's base plate so the blade will be in the center. Make a plunge cut to pass the blade through the insert, then screw the saw's base plate to the insert *(left)*. If there are fewer than four screw holes in the base plate, drill additional holes.

Mount the drill and saber saw inserts to the cleats as you would the router insert.

Make the fence the same way you would for the router table on page 135, and attach it in the desired position with clamps.

Building a benchtop router table

The benchtop table shown above is a full-size router table with most of the features of the manufactured version, including a pivoting, quickly adjustable fence. Begin by cutting the top from ³⁄₄-inch plywood, sized to suit your needs; the table illustrated measures 24 by 36 inches. The four top rails should next be cut from 1-by-2 stock and screwed in place (countersinking all screws, here and in future steps), and the entire top should be covered with a piece of ¹⁄₄-inch plastic laminate, chamfered at the edges. Turn the table over so you can screw supports around the inside edges and attach the legs to the rails and top. The supports, legs, and feet can be constructed of ³⁄₄-inch plywood; the final dimensions will be determined by the size of your table. Make sure the legs are at least long enough to furnish ample room for your router. To prepare the tabletop for the router, drill a hole about 8 inches from the front center; make it slightly larger than your largest router bit. On the underside of the top, center the router over the hole and trace its outline. Use the router to plow a ¹⁄₄-inch recess within the outline to accommodate your router base plate (or, make an acrylic sub-base and mount it as shown on page 137). Mark the location of the base plate screw holes, drill counterbore holes, and you will be ready to fasten the router in place. Next, construct the fence (about 6 inches longer than the top) out of two pieces of 1-by-3 stock screwed together in the form of an L.

Through the base of the L, drill a hole for a ¹⁄₄-inch carriage bolt about six inches from one end. Now center the fence about 6 inches from the rear of the top, mark the position of the hole, and drill for the carriage bolt. Slip a bolt through the hole; using that as a pivot, swing the right end of the fence forward. When the fence reaches the hole you cut for the router bit, mark the hole's position on the fence. That is where you will cut a clearance notch to accommodate your largest router bit. Make a guard that is hinged so it will swing out of the way like the one shown on page 136. Screw your router to the top and assemble the fence by inserting the carriage bolt from the bottom, using washers and wing nuts to tighten it. Adjust the fence for any width of work by pivoting it into place and securing the free end with a C clamp.

GLOSSARY

A-B-C

Bench dog: A round or square peg of metal or wood that fits into a hole in a workbench to grip and hold a workpiece in place.

Bevel cut: A cut at an angle from face to face along the length or width of a workpiece.

Box joint: Identical interlocking fingers that mesh to form a corner joint.

Butt joinery: A method of joining wood in which the end or edge of one board is set squarely against the face or edge of another.

Carcase: A box-like construction that constitutes the body of a piece of furniture.

Cheek: The face of the projecting tenon in a mortise-and-tenon joint.

Circuit: Continuous path for electrical current; from the main service panel in a house or garage, a branch circuit runs to a series of outlets, wall switches, and light fixtures, and returns to the panel.

Counterbore: To drill a hole that permits the head of a screw or bolt to sit below a wood surface so it can be concealed by a wood plug.

Countersink: To drill a hole so that the head of a screw or bolt will lie flush with or slightly below the surface of a workpiece.

Crosscut: A saw cut across the wood grain of a workpiece.

D-E-F

Dado: A rectangular channel cut into a workpiece.

Decibel: The standard measuring unit of sound intensity; the decibel (db) scale extends from 0 to about 130, with 0 representing barely perceptible sounds and 130 delineating the average pain level.

Dedicated circuit: An electrical circuit to which only one tool or fixture is connected.

Dovetail joinery: A method of joining wood at corners by means of interlocking pins and tails; the name is derived from the distinctive shape cut into the ends of the joining boards.

Dowel: A wood pin used to reinforce certain types of wood joints.

End cap: A piece of wood that covers each end of the top slab of a workbench; bolted to the slab and glued to the aprons by means of dovetail or finger joints.

Face gluing: Bonding several boards together face-to-face to form a thicker workpiece.

Face jointing: Using a jointer to cut shavings from the face of a workpiece until it is flat and square with the edge.

Face vise: A vise that holds work against the front apron of a workbench.

Featherboard: A piece of wood cut with thin fingers or "feathers" at one end; used in conjunction with clamps to hold a workpiece secure against the fence or table of a power tool.

Fence: An adjustable guide designed to keep the edge or face of a workpiece a fixed distance from the cutting edge of a tool.

Furring strip: A thin board that is nailed to a wall or ceiling to provide a flat or level surface for securing drywall or paneling.

G-H-I-J

Ground-fault circuit interrupter (GFCI): A type of electrical outlet that trips instantly when it detects a short-circuit leak in current.

Hanger bolt: A bolt with no head; one end of the bolt has screw threads while the other end features machine threads.

Inlay: A decorative strip of metal, hardwood, or marquetry that is glued in a groove cut into a workpiece.

Joist: A horizontal support for a floor.

K-L

Kerf: A cut made in wood by the thickness of a saw blade.

Kerf splitter: A metal device that holds a kerf slightly open during a saw cut to prevent the blade from binding.

Kickback: The tendency of a workpiece to be thrown back in the direction of the operator of a power tool.

Knockdown fitting: A piece of hardware that accepts a screw or bolt, allowing the quick assembly and disassembly of a workbench or other furniture.

Lap joint: A type of joint in which matching dadoes or rabbets overlap to connect two boards.

Lead anchor: A type of fitting that is inserted into a hole in concrete or masonry; expands to hold a screw or bolt securely.

Leg vise: A vise that secures stock to the front left-hand leg of a workbench.

M-N-O-P-Q-R-S

Miter cut: A cut that angles across the face of a workpiece.

Mortise: A rectangular, round, or oval-shaped hole cut into a piece of wood.

Mortise-and-tenon: A joint in which a projecting tenon on one board fits into a mortise on another.

Push block or stick: A device used to feed a workpiece into the blade, cutterhead, or bit of a tool to protect the operator's fingers.

Rabbet: A step-like cut in the edge or end of a workpiece; usually forms part of a joint.

Rail: A board running along the bottom edge of a tabletop to which the legs of a table can be attached.

Service entrance: A box containing circuit breakers or fuses, from which power is distributed to house branch circuits.

Shoulder: In a mortise-and-tenon joint, the part of the tenon that is perpendicular to the cheek.

Shoulder vise: A fixed type of face vise with a jaw that moves to clamp a workpiece against the front apron of a workbench.

Sliding dog block: A wood block, part of the tail vise of a workbench, that applies the clamping face to hold a workpiece between the bench dogs.

Static pressure: A measure of the friction encountered by air as it moves through a duct; often expressed in inches per foot.

Stretcher: A board running between the legs of a workbench to provide additional support.

Stud: A vertical member forming walls and supporting the framework of a building.

T-U-V-W-X-Y-Z

Tail vise: A screw-type vise on the right-hand end of a workbench incorporating a sliding dog block to secure stock on the top surface of the bench.

Tenon: A protrusion from the end of a board that fits into a mortise.

Truing: Squaring the end of a blade or the working surface of a grinder wheel so that it conforms to its original shape.

Truss rod: A type of threaded metal rod used to reinforce the legs and stretchers of a workbench.

Wheel dresser: A star-wheel or diamond-point device used to true the working surface of a grinding wheel and expose fresh abrasive particles.

INDEX

Page references in *italics* indicate an illustration of subject matter. Page references in **bold** indicate a Build It Yourself project.

ACKNOWLEDGMENTS

The editors wish to thank the following:

SAFETY

Adjustable Clamp Co., Chicago, IL; Black & Decker/Elu Power Tools, Towson, MD; Delta International Machinery/Porter Cable, Guelph, Ont.; Fisher Hill Products, Inc., Fitzwilliam, NH; Freud Westmore Tools, Ltd., Mississauga, Ont.; Lee Valley Tools Ltd., Ottawa, Ont.; Sears, Roebuck and Co., Chicago, IL; Vermont American Corp., Lincolnton, NC and Louisville, KY

SHOP LAYOUT

Black & Decker Power Tools, Towson, MD; Delta International Machinery/Porter Cable, Guelph, Ont.; Hitachi Power Tools U.S.A. Ltd., Norcross, GA; Lee Valley Tools Ltd., Ottawa, Ont.; Sears, Roebuck and Co., Chicago, IL; Thoroughbred Sawhorses and Equipment, Division of the Ivy Group, Inc., Valparaiso, IN

WORKBENCH

Adjustable Clamp Co., Chicago, IL; Black & Decker/Elu Power Tools, Towson, MD; Delta International Machinery/Porter Cable, Guelph, Ont.; Freud Westmore Tools, Ltd., Mississauga, Ont.; Great Neck Saw Mfrs. Inc. (Buck Bros. Division), Millbury, MA; Hitachi Power Tools U.S.A. Ltd., Norcross, GA; Lee Valley Tools Ltd., Ottawa, Ont.; Record Tools Inc., Pickering, Ont.; Robert Larson Company, Inc., San Francisco, CA; Sandvik Saws and Tools Co., Scranton, PA; Sears, Roebuck and Co., Chicago, IL; Thoroughbred Sawhorses and Equipment, Division of the Ivy Group, Inc., Valparaiso, IN; Vermont American Corp., Lincolnton, NC and Louisville, KY

SHOP ACCESSORIES

Campbell Hausfeld, Harrison, OH; Delta International Machinery/Porter Cable, Guelph, Ont.; Dewalt Industrial Tool Co., Hampstead, MD; Great Neck Saw Mfrs. Inc. (Buck Bros. Division), Millbury, MA; Ingersoll-Rand Canada Inc., Rexdale, Ont.; Sears, Roebuck and Co., Chicago, IL; Wagner Spray Tech Corp., Minneapolis, MN

STORAGE

Adjustable Clamp Co., Chicago, IL; American Tool Cos., Lincoln, NE; Freud Westmore Tools, Ltd., Mississauga, Ont.; Hitachi Power Tools U.S.A. Ltd., Norcross, GA; Lee Valley Tools Ltd., Ottawa, Ont.; Robert Sorby Ltd., Sheffield, U.K./Busy Bee Machine Tools, Concord, Ont.; Sandvik Saws and Tools Co., Scranton, PA; Stanley Tools, Division of the Stanley Works, New Britain, CT; Vermont American Corp., Lincolnton, NC and Louisville, KY

WORK SURFACES

Adjustable Clamp Co., Chicago, IL; Black & Decker Power Tools, Towson, MD; Delta International Machinery/Porter Cable, Guelph, Ont.; Freud Westmore Tools, Ltd., Mississauga, Ont.; Hitachi Power Tools U.S.A. Ltd., Norcross, GA; Lee Valley Tools Ltd., Ottawa, Ont.; Record Tools Inc., Pickering, Ont.; Sandvik Saws and Tools Co., Scranton, PA; Sears, Roebuck and Co., Chicago, IL; Shopsmith, Inc., Montreal, Que.; Stanley Tools, Division of the Stanley Works, New Britain, CT; Thoroughbred Sawhorses and Equipment, Division of the Ivy Group, Inc., Valparaiso, IN; Tru-Align Manufacturing Inc., Tempe, AZ; Vermont American Corp., Lincolnton, NC and Louisville, KY

The following persons also assisted in the preparation of this book:

René Bertrand, Elizabeth Cameron, Donna Curtis, Lorraine Doré, Réjean Garand, Graphor Consultation, Irene Huang, Carolyn Jackson, Leonard Lee, Geneviève Monette

PICTURE CREDITS

Cover Robert Chartier
6, 7 Robert Holmes
8, 9 Raymond Gendreau
10, 11 Ron Levine
30 Courtesy Shopsmith, Inc.
47 Courtesy Sjöbergs of Sweden
49 Courtesy Woodcraft Supply Corp.
70 Courtesy Makita Canada Ltd.
89 Courtesy Justrite Manufacturing Co.
112 (upper) Courtesy Shure Manufacturing Corp.